GIMME MY MONEY BACK
Your Guide to Beating the Financial Crisis

by Ali Velshi

Sterling & Ross Publishers
NEW YORK

Published by
Sterling & Ross Publishers
New York, NY 10001
www.SterlingandRoss.com

Contributing Editor: Thomas Wynbrandt

Cover design: Chris Stribley © Nederpelt Media
Cover photo: Mark Hill © 2008 Cable News Network, A Time Warner Co. All rights reserved.
Project Editor/Book design: Rachel Trusheim
Special thanks to Ibbotson Associates and Morningstar for graphics and data, used with permission, © 2008 Morningstar, Inc.

Library of Congress Cataloging-in-Publication Data

Velshi, Ali.
  Gimme my money back : your guide to beating the finanicial crisis / by Ali Velshi.
    p. cm.
  ISBN 978-0-9814535-6-9 (pbk.)
  1. Financial crises. 2. Recessions. 3. Finance, Personal. I. Title.
  HB3722.V45 2009
  332.024--dc22
                          2008051560

10 9 8 7 6 5 4 3 2 1

Printed in the United States of America.

"Money makes the world go around, the world go around, the world go around…"

— John Kander and Fred Ebb, *Cabaret*

TABLE OF CONTENTS

PREFACE

I f you're reading this book, then you've already taken a first step toward securing your financial future.

You've made a decision to build wealth. You're prepared to seize the opportunities available to you. You want to learn more about money—how it works, how it grows and what you should do.

That's why I wrote this book.

Gimme My Money Back is designed to empower you to make the right financial choices for you, your family and your future. It's packed with information, tools and guidance to help you help yourself.

This book is focused on one thing: how to make money in the markets. It's not about your credit or annuities or the other aspects of your life. My only goal is helping you succeed as an investor.

As the chief business correspondent for CNN, I read your emails and I take your calls every day. I know that too many of you are struggling to make ends meet. But there is a way out—it's investing.

More than half of all working Americans invest in the stock market, mainly though voluntary defined contribution plans like 401(k)s, 403(b)s or IRAs. Although you likely don't see yourself as an investor, you probably are.

You didn't cause this financial crisis. So if you've been hammered, it's not surprising if you feel that someone took your money. Let me tell you this: whether you're a first-timer or an experienced investor, this book can help you get it back.

There are a lot of changes taking place in our economy and our world. But change means opportunity. And I'll show you how to take advantage of those opportunities, starting now.

In this book, you'll learn:

1. What caused the financial crisis of 2008.

2. The unseen role that credit and banking play in your life.

3. Why some debt can be good, why some debt is bad and how to tell the difference between the two.

4. Why you should invest, and what your investment choices are.

5. Five easy-to-understand principles that drive investment success.

6. The smart, proven ways to build your investment portfolio.

7. How to structure a portfolio for your individual situation.

8. The strategies that will help you build a solid retirement.

I'll help you understand risk, and why the greatest risk is doing nothing. And we'll survey the world of financial planners to determine if one might be right for you.

We all have reasons to invest: retirement, our children's education, a new house, that dream vacation, or simply to relax on the front porch free of worry. But no matter how different our dreams might be, they all require a solid financial foundation to make them a reality. That's what this book is all about.

Whatever your age or financial status, you'll find common sense advice and explanations to help make you a smarter, savvier investor. You'll get targeted, actionable information you can use right away.

At the end of *Gimme My Money Back*, you'll even find a series of model investment portfolios. The minute you finish this book, you can take them to your 401(k) or IRA and begin making the changes that will bring you a better future.

Remember, it's never too late to begin an investment plan, and there's never been a better time to start. Invest your time in this book and it will pay dividends. You'll be wiser, better informed and better equipped to take control of your financial life.

Ali Velshi

1 | WHAT HAPPENED?

"The stock market is but a mirror which... provides an image of the underlying or fundamental economic situation."

— John Kenneth Galbraith (1908-2006)

I f you had waved good-bye to Earth at the end of 2007 and returned at the beginning of 2009, you might not recognize the old place. The robust U.S. economy you left is mired in near-record unemployment. Major investment banks, run by the smartest guys in the world, have collapsed, dragging their shareholders down with them. The housing market is in ruins, banks have failed, federal agencies are drowning and money is hemorrhaging from the U.S. financial system. Trillions—not billions, trillions—have been lost.

It's a global crisis, and the pain's going to last a long time. Like a mountaineering accident in which everyone's roped together on the icy slope—suddenly, one person loses his balance and tumbles over the edge. Then, the next in line, caught unawares, drops from sight before he has time to set his ice axe. Soon the weight of the free-falling climbers pulls the entire party to its doom.

Only here, imagine that the heaviest, largest mountaineer, someone much bigger than the others, is the first one to go over. And he's not roped to only one line of climbers, he's somehow roped to five or six, all of them taking slightly different routes to the top and all somehow linked to the others. Because in today's world, the hip bone isn't just connected to the thigh bone. The smallest bit of market information can be wired to a data center in India that's linked to high-speed transmitters in Switzerland routed via a satellite that's beaming information to China, Brazil, Russia, Spain and South Africa from its geosynchronous orbit above the equator. And it's all happening at the speed of light.

How did we get here?

By now you've probably heard that this global credit crisis was precipitated by the sub-prime lending mess, but what does that mean? Whose fault is it? Greedy banks? Predatory lenders? Regulators asleep at the switch? Wall Street? Who is to blame? Where is justice?

The truth is there's plenty of blame to go around. Banks, mortgage companies and Wall Street all played a part. The government could have done more, and acted sooner, than it did. But we, as individuals, bear some responsibility, too.

We enjoyed our culture of immediate gratification. We didn't save; we borrowed. We placed too much reliance on credit and we became too comfortable with debt. Yes, Wall Street investment firms bought too many complex derivatives without fully vetting the value of their underlying assets. But back on Main Street, many of us accepted loans we didn't really understand just because the banks were more than willing to give them to us. Those loans helped finance our dreams.

Some killjoys talked about a housing bubble, but we didn't want to listen, did we? Times were good—credit was easy, our houses were worth more every day and we wanted to believe they'd keep appreciating forever.

But as we all know, bubbles burst. When it happens with bubble gum, one person gets it on the face. When it happens in the economy, we all have to deal with some part of the mess.

Still, though, the question remains: how did a relatively small percentage of people who couldn't make their mortgage payments morph into the second biggest financial crisis the U.S. has ever faced? Let's take a look back, to when things really began to go haywire.

Nineteen days of hell

From the start, 2008 had not been a banner year. The market had hit an all-time high of 14,164 on October 9, 2007 and had fallen more or less steadily since then. By July 2, 2008, it was down 20 percent—official bear market territory. But worse, much worse, was coming.

On Sunday, September 14, 2008, Lehman Brothers, the venerable Wall Street investment bank, went under. In dollar terms, it was a failure five times bigger than the largest previous bankruptcy. The same day, Merrill Lynch, the largest brokerage firm in the world, a name known in every town in every state, had to sell itself to Bank of America to avoid potential bankruptcy. And Wall Street, dizzy at what it had just seen, didn't know what might be coming next.

The very next day, Wall Street found out. A.I.G., the world's biggest insurance company, was close to collapse. Agencies were threatening to lower the firm's credit rating: if that happened, it could trigger a series of events that would have forced it out of business. A.I.G., with insurance contracts that touched just about every major business around the globe, desperately needed to raise $40 billion.

Remember, this was a Monday. Investors had held their breath all weekend; now they were in full panic. Lehman was gone, Merrill was gone, A.I.G. teetered on the edge, losing 60 percent of its value during the day. In droves, investors fled the stock market. The Dow fell 504 points.

On Tuesday, September 16, the government rode to the rescue. A.I.G., which had been on the hook for billions in potential losses stemming from complex transactions, gratefully accepted an infusion of $85 billion to continue its operations. In exchange for the cash, the government took a large stake in the company.

The drama continued on Wednesday. The markets saw a "flight to quality," as risky assets were dumped in favor of those with lower, but more certain, returns. With money pouring out of stocks and into safe havens, the Dow dropped another 449 points. Gold saw its biggest one-day gain in 10 years.

With trust in the system non-existent, we saw a nearly

complete freeze of credit. Banks didn't trust other banks to be able to repay loans. Even customers with good credit were rejected. When companies were able to borrow money, they paid twice as much in interest as they had paid only days earlier. Like a car running out of oil, credit—the engine of our financial system—was seizing up. No one had the courage to lend money; no one was sure that any borrower could pay it back.

The only institution with sufficient capital and sufficient clout to get things moving again was the federal government. On Thursday, September 18, Secretary of the Treasury Henry Paulson met with congressional leaders from both major political parties and laid out for them, in plain and direct language, just how dire the situation was.

He told the congressmen and senators that, absent a massive infusion of cash, the country was careening toward the kind of financial calamity not seen since the Great Depression. He said that the time for investigations and blame assessment would have to come later; the immediate priority had to be keeping conditions from worsening.

And the way to do that, he said, was to pass a rescue package that would commit more than $700 billion to shoring up the nation's financial and banking systems. Even in Washington, a city accustomed to large numbers, it was a staggering amount of money.

I was in the CNN studio during those days, following every nuance of every development as it unfolded. The speed and ferocity of the meltdown astonished experienced journalists and Wall Streeters alike. The stock market was dropping off a cliff. Good companies were facing doom. I spoke with seasoned financiers in New York and veteran reporters in Washington: no one had ever seen anything like it. And with each new revelation, we all looked at one another and wondered, "What's next?"

Over the next twelve days, as the administration and Congress went back and forth over the wisdom of the plan, its particulars and its political ramifications, the financial world continued its fevered shudders. Goldman Sachs and Morgan Stanley, the only two stand-alone investment banks left on Wall Street, threw in the towel and agreed to become bank holding companies, subject to more restrictive regulations on their activities. It was as though two tough gunslingers in the Old West had decided to become farmers. Maybe it wasn't as exciting a profession, but given the current climate and the likely future, it was a lot safer. And once Goldman and Morgan hung up their holsters, investment banking as we knew it was dead.

As the situation spiraled downward, the government seized Washington Mutual, the largest home mortgage issuer in the country and sold it to JPMorgan Chase. The bank had been instrumental in creating and selling sub-prime loans; now, like Baron Frankenstein, its monster had turned on it. Wachovia, the nation's fourth largest financial services firm in terms of assets, was also in trouble. Faced with two eager suitors intent on picking it up on the cheap, it went with Wells Fargo, leaving Citigroup stunned at the altar.

Throughout the weekend of September 27 and 28, Secretary Paulson and Ben Bernanke, the chairman of the Federal Reserve Board, lobbied reluctant lawmakers, trying to sell their plan. They believed—they *knew*—it was right. A healthy, robust adult had suffered a heart attack, they said. The $700 billion was the electric shock that would get the heart beating again. Administer the shock and the patient will recover fully, they said. Without it, he will die.

But Congress wasn't about to give the Treasury Department what it called a "blank check." Where were the controls? Where was the oversight? How can you give us a three-page document when you're asking us for $700 billion? It's arrogant, said Congress. The battle raged.

On Monday, September 29, after reports that a tentative deal had been reached in Congress, the rescue plan was shockingly voted down. It probably didn't help that it was called a "bailout" rather than a rescue. America was horrified. The Dow plunged another 778 points. Paulson and Bernanke redoubled their efforts.

Then on Wednesday, October 1, after intense ideological arguments, the Emergency Economic Stabilization Act of 2008 passed the Senate. On Friday, October 3, the House fell into line. Now it was official: the government would buy troubled assets from the banks. No one was particularly happy. Some conservatives saw government climbing into bed with private enterprise and felt we had taken the first step down the road to socialism. Some liberals saw $700 billion that could have been used for schools, health care and other social programs fly away. But in the end, lawmakers realized that the only alternative to passing the bill was letting the crisis spread like a strange virus, freezing everything in its path. Despite their misgivings about the bill, they couldn't let that happen.

Their reward for making the tough decision? The market fell another 157 points that day.

Many economists believe that the full effects of our current problems haven't been felt yet. It's hurting Wall Street, they say, but on Main Street the pain's just beginning. Hard to believe when we lost more than two million jobs in 2008 alone. Hard to believe when we're looking at home foreclosure rates that haven't been seen since the Great Depression. Sobering when we see the millions of Americans who have had their pensions cut, their health insurance cancelled, their retirement savings wiped out.

But it will likely get worse. In October 2008, consumer spending fell for the first time in 17 years. People out of work don't spend money. People who fear for their jobs don't spend much either. And when people buy less—be it clothes, food, carpet, vacations, whatever—then the companies that sell those things don't do very well. When they have to lay off employees because they can't afford to pay them, the system is caught in a self-reinforcing spiral of decline.

The spiral began, we know, with the sub-prime mortgage lending mess. Like many bad situations, it looked good at the beginning.

Sub-prime mortgage: the backstory

A little history is in order here. It used to be very difficult to buy a house. Banks had strict lending policies, often demanding a down payment of at least 30 percent, a solid work history and monthly mortgage payments that were no more than 30 percent of adjusted gross income.

If, despite the bank's rigorous due diligence, the borrower defaulted on the mortgage, the bank foreclosed, took control of the home and tried to sell it someone else. The bank didn't like being in the real estate business; it wanted to stay in the banking business. So it only lent money to people it considered very, very safe. And it only gave mortgages on homes that met equally stringent criteria.

But over the past 30 years, we began to emphasize home ownership as a kind of national goal. According to this creed, people who owned their homes had a greater stake in their communities, their families and themselves. By building equity in their homes, owners automatically had a financial self-interest in building a better neighborhood. Ownership led to better citizenship, proponents said, because it gave people the incentive to improve the community. No one doubted that helping families own their own homes was a worthy goal.

To help make that goal a reality, banks and mortgage companies were encouraged to relax their lending standards. They were given certain incentives to grant mortgages to people with sketchier work histories or less sterling credit records than had previously been required. They were asked to lower down payment requirements. To cover the added risk that some of the new mortgage applicants represented, the banks were allowed to charge higher interest rates for these loans. They also received credits for their participation in the Community Reinvestment Act, the federal program that promoted mortgages for first-time homebuyers who previously would not have qualified for them.

On the whole, these programs were phenomenally successful. First-time homeowners did, as hoped, help to re-build communities. They were committed to their homes and their neighborhoods. They revived failing schools and turned weed-strewn lots into new parks. Studies showed that homeowners spent more time with their children, worked harder and more successfully at their jobs and spent more on the upkeep of their properties than did renters.[1]

The programs worked for the banks, too. They had found a great way to reduce the risk of the loans they gave to the less qualified: they sold those loans.

The banks had always been able to sell mortgage loans to two quasi-public agencies: the Federal National Mortgage Association (Fannie Mae) and the Federal Home Loan Mortgage Corporation (Freddie Mac). By purchasing the bank's mortgages, Fannie and Freddie kept the supply of capital—money—flowing to the banks so that they could make more loans. In other words, Fannie and Freddie helped to provide liquidity to the system.

But now new players arrived on the scene to buy the banks' loans. These firms, along with Fannie and Freddie, bundled together multiple mortgages and sold them in $100 million slices, called tranches, to institutions that then re-sold smaller slices as investments to other institutions in turn. Each tranche had its own unique set of risk parameters depending upon the mortgages it contained, and each was priced accordingly.

Basically, each buyer was purchasing a percentage of the revenue stream from the mortgage payments. The most stable mortgages paid the least, as the highest-quality borrowers had been able to obtain the most favorable terms. At the other end of the scale, mortgages given to the most questionable borrowers paid the most, as these were the loans deemed most likely to default.

In a fast-motion sketch, it might go something like this:

Say the bank gives a 6 percent mortgage to Annie, using her house as collateral. Every month, the bank gets its 6 percent interest. Then, in its quest for more money, the bank turns around and sells the monthly revenue stream from that mortgage to Fannie or Freddie or Wall Street, keeping a small percentage for itself. So now every month, Wall Street gets 5 percent, the bank gets 1 percent and Annie keeps paying her mortgage and living in her house.

Then Fannie and Freddie and Wall Street decide to do what the bank did. But they don't sell just one mortgage. They marry thousands of them together into $100 million bundles called mortgage bonds and sell these bonds to investors around the world—foreign governments, hedge funds, you name it. These bondholders get, say, 4 percent. The original bank keeps its 1 percent, Wall Street keeps 1 percent, Annie stays in her house. It all works great; everybody's happy. But then interest rates go up.

Annie can't make the new payments. The bank repossesses the house. But now it's not worth as much as the mortgage the bank gave her in the first place. The same thing happens to Annies all over the country. And the system that allowed everybody to make money off the same mortgage collapses. The bank has to repossess all those houses and put them on sale. And the bank discovers that they really aren't worth much anymore.

Many other hardworking people were caught in the foreclosure net. People like Mark, for example. He's a good guy. He's got a steady job, some savings and a good credit score. He went to the bank to borrow $50,000 toward the purchase of a $200,000 home, at a 30-year fixed rate of 6 percent. That would have cost him about $300 a month, something he could afford.

But his bank had a better plan. Mark had picked out a good house in a good neighborhood, and the bank expects the house to increase in value. So the bank's willing to loan him 80 percent of the purchase price—$160,000! Mark only needs to put $40,000 down, and he can use the money he saved for other things.

Now, obviously, the payments on $160,000 are going to be higher, but the interest rate is going to be lower! Four percent. It's called a "teaser" rate. Not for the life of the loan, but for the first year. After that it re-adjusts, but nobody thinks rates are going up. So Mark walks out with a much bigger loan than he thought he could afford, with a much bigger monthly payment—$765 instead of $300. But he now has $110,000 in cash he didn't use. Some of it can go toward the increased monthly payments, and some can be used for other things—like a renovation, maybe?

Poor Mark. He walked into the bank as a "prime borrower" and walked out "sub-prime." His new debt-to-asset ratio automatically made him a higher risk. The bank—assured that he has a good job, a good credit history and a house that will increase in value—offered him a loan he probably shouldn't have taken and, one way or another, he agreed to it.

The scene was now set for a fall. And though the collapse, when it came, unfolded rapidly, the seeds of the problem had been planted a decade earlier.

The gathering storm

Starting in the late 1990s, home prices began to appreciate quickly. In virtually all cities, in almost all neighborhoods, houses, condos and apartments soared in value. With interest rates low and down payment requirements often no more than 2 percent, people were able to afford bigger loans than they thought. And the banks had an interest in pushing people into bigger loans: the banks made more money on them. That was because the bigger the loan, the more it cost the borrower, because of the higher potential risk.

If a bank could offer a $50,000 mortgage at 6 percent or a $100,000 mortgage at 8 percent, it didn't take much persuasion to convince a couple that the $100,000 mortgage was the right move. Didn't you really love that more expensive house? And the way housing prices are going, you'll probably be able to double your money in a few years and move into something better still! Meanwhile, we'll just put your mortgage together with these others here and sell 90 percent of the revenue stream to an institution planning to keep a portion of their portion and add a commission to the rest of it and sell it to a hedge fund…

Some borrowers decided to refinance. After all, their homes were now worth much more than they had been. So the homeowners could get new mortgages at lower interest rates or, even better, take out second mortgages against the added value in their homes. They could use this money for anything—home improvement, for example. But many people opted simply to go shopping with it. With this sort of mindset, multiplied by millions of borrowers, household debt doubled, going from $7 trillion in 2001 to $14 trillion in 2008.[2]

Another seemingly benign financing option was the adjustable rate mortgage (ARM), eagerly promoted by banks. These mortgages allowed homeowners to pay very low interest during an initial period, not unlike an introductory offer on a credit card. Some ARM loans allowed people to pay only the interest, not the principal, during this period. Often the initial rate was less than 4 percent—but it could increase significantly once the teaser period was over. Sometimes the monthly payment more than doubled.

Eventually, the spinning top started to wobble on its axis. Builders had rushed to erect new housing to take advantage of the boom; now various regions of the country were overbuilt. People weren't buying the new homes. By late 2007, those homes started to pile up. Construction workers were laid off. The economy began to slow.

Remember Mark? He was feeling a little stressed. Sometime in the last year, he'd found all sorts of things to do with the "extra" $110,000 he suddenly had. He'd made some stylish renovations, but it wasn't enough to boost the value of his home in a falling market. And his "teaser" rate had expired; he was now paying around 7 percent. His $765 monthly payment jumped to $1,065.

As housing prices fell, it suddenly became more difficult

to refinance. Then interest rates began to climb. Mark and others who had agreed to adjustable-rate mortgages began to feel squeezed, then strangled. The system began to spin out of control.

Mark missed a payment, and it cost him. His interest rate jumped to 8 percent—$1,175 a month. He knew he couldn't afford the new payment and he tried to sell his house. But everyone around him was doing the same thing, and all it did was push prices down. Many people found themselves with mortgages that suddenly bore no relationship to the value of their homes. Why keep paying off a $200,000 home when it's now only worth $160,000? Why not just walk away? Mark was just one of millions of homeowners who, unable to sell or to refinance at lower rates, began to default on their loans.

Uh-oh

By March 2008, more than 10 percent of all homeowners had homes that were "upside down"—worth less than their mortgages.[3] The first to fail were the sub-primes. They had always been the riskiest, so it was expected that they'd have the most trouble in a downturn. After all, by definition, a sub-prime loan was a loan that failed to meet the standards for a prime loan. That's why lenders could charge more interest, to cover the higher risk of default. Now default was here. What was once abstract had become concrete.

But the problem was much broader than had been anticipated. Because it wasn't just the lower-middle-class worker, recently laid off, who was suddenly in default. It was also the college-educated couple in white collar professions who had allowed the bank to put them in a house they really couldn't afford, on the assumption that property values would keep rising forever. It was the retiree who bought the place on the golf course just before the rise in gasoline prices made the drive there prohibitively expensive and put the whole condo development into receivership. Surveying the broken landscape, it was clear that the *people* weren't sub-prime; it was simply that a whole swath of the public had been pushed, cajoled or tempted into borrowing more money than circumstances deemed prudent.

And as property values tumbled ever lower, the investment banks and others who had bought those revenue streams from mortgages that had been re-packaged and sold to them began to realize that they had no way to assess the real value of the investments they were now stuck with. What mortgages, exactly, were in those packages? How much would the underlying property be worth right now? How can we figure it out?

Until that moment, those mortgages had been solid investments with reliable returns. Now financial institutions that had always borrowed against the value of their mortgage pools suddenly discovered that with no accurate way to value them, those mortgages were worthless as collateral. Even big banks run on credit. With a constant need for borrowed money, they were in big trouble.

Some buyers of these re-packaged mortgages had tried to protect themselves by purchasing insurance against possible default, using something called credit default swaps.

Credit default swaps are not regulated by any government

agency. They are agreements between two parties. They operate, in effect, as a "shadow" credit market. It was A.I.G.'s role as an issuer of credit default swaps that came close to forcing it over the edge. Having agreed to insure other firms against credit default, and with defaults on the rise, A.I.G. realized that it didn't have enough cash on hand to cover the payments it might have to make if everyone demanded his or her money at the same time. Just like the old days of runs on the bank.

Could these companies meet their debt obligations? No one could say. The situation grew increasingly murky. Without confidence, without trust, there could be no credit. And without credit, it's very difficult to do business.

And there was about to be no credit.

2 | CREDIT WHERE CREDIT IS DUE

"Money alone sets all the world in motion."

— Livy (59 B.C.-A.D. 17)

The world runs on credit. The grocery store, the clothing manufacturer, the "big box" retailer, even you and I depend on credit in our everyday lives. Credit implies faith in the future because, at heart, the idea is, "I'll pay you tomorrow for what you give me today." The institution most associated with extending credit is, of course, the bank.

Jet fuel for business

The larger a business is, the more credit it is likely to need. A home appliance manufacturer, for example, depends on the sale of dishwashers and refrigerators for income. But it costs plenty of money to make those things in the first place. The manufacturer has to buy steel and other components. There are factories full of workers to be paid. The factory is filled with the latest robotic assembly machines, expensive tools controlled by programmable chips that reduce the cost of manufacturing by some slight amount over each unit produced. The factory itself is a hulking behemoth of brick, metal and glass with a mortgage on it, held by a bank. When dishwashers, refrigerators, washers and dryers are ready for sale, the manufacturer must pay to get them to stores in every corner of every continent (except Antarctica).

No manufacturer—not Whirlpool, not GE, not Sanyo nor Panasonic, none of them—has sufficient cash on hand to fund every aspect of such a sprawling, capital-intensive operation. So the company borrows money to cover its manufacturing, labor, distribution and promotion costs, and recoups the expenses when it sells its many products. This is Business 101, a standard paradigm followed over and over throughout the world.

And if we delve deeper into the manufacturer's world, we'll see that its way of working is replicated in the activities of its suppliers. The mills that make the aluminum and sheet steel for the appliances borrow money to buy the iron ore, carbon, manganese and other elements needed to produce the metal to the manufacturer's specifications. And the companies mining the metals borrow to pay their workers, to lease the ships that transport the ore, to buy those giant, mountain-eating steam shovels that rip the ore from the ground. People won't wait forever for money; almost everyone has to pay suppliers before he gets paid himself. The same holds true for the company that makes the electronic assemblies for the earth-moving machines, or the computer chips that run the coffee makers, or the plastic wire baskets that sit inside the dishwashers.

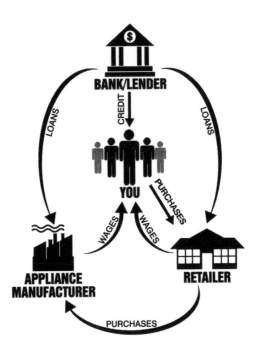

In the illustration, the bank, like the sun, helps everything grow. The bank loans money to you for your needs, to the manufacturer for his and to the retailer for hers. The retailer spends some of that borrowed money to purchase products from the manufacturer, products she will sell to you. The manufacturer uses the borrowed money to pay suppliers, distributors and labor costs until he gets the money back in sales. You may use borrowed money to pay for your house or car. You also receive wages from your job. Maybe you're an employee of the manufacturer or the retailer, or maybe you're in another industry altogether. In any case, those wages allow you to pay back the bank and to purchase the goods and services you need for everyday living.

All over the globe, we witness the same phenomenon: money is loaned to promote economic activity on the promise of future payment. If banks refused to believe that promise, if they refused to lend money, then business as we know it would cease to exist.

It was just this breakdown in confidence that came close to causing an economic death plunge in the waning months of 2008. Banks stopped trusting their customers. They had no faith in repayment. The flow of credit—the lubricant that allowed the system to function smoothly—dried up. And if the system had stopped, it would have been very, very difficult to get it moving again.

That, in a nutshell, is what happened during the credit crisis of 2008.

Everyone, from Washington to Wall Street to the Federal Reserve to central banks around the world, has taken action to try to deal with this credit crisis. Only time will tell whether those actions will work. For you, the toll has been heavy and there's not a moment to lose. The job now is to go forward, to realize that this is the absolute best moment to take the steps needed to build wealth smartly, and to thank our lucky stars that, despite it all, we still have many, many opportunities to prosper.

Bank on it

Since we've just been discussing credit, let's take a look at the way banks work. Despite the growth of credit unions, private equity firms and other non-traditional sources of financing, banks are far and away the country's primary source of funding for businesses and individuals.

Banks accept your deposits and pay interest on the money you give them for safekeeping. They promise to give your money back when you ask for it or on a pre-determined date. At the same time, they loan the money you've given them to individuals and businesses in the community. They charge interest to these borrowers, an interest that's higher than the interest they pay to depositors. The difference between the interest they charge borrowers and the interest they pay to depositors is primarily how they make their money.

Prior to the Great Depression in the 1930s, your bank deposit was not insured by the federal government. If your bank went out of business, you lost every cent you had deposited. In tough economic times, this happened regularly. There were agencies in certain states that insured state banks that adhered to a rigid set of requirements, but the system was piecemeal and largely ineffective.

All it took was the rumor that a bank was short of funds and frightened depositors ran to the bank and demanded their money on the spot. Very few institutions had the resources on hand to pay off each and every depositor. If the institution wasn't bankrupt before, it was then.

This is what happens in the classic Christmas movie, *It's*

a Wonderful Life. Jimmy Stewart, the actor playing the part of small savings and loan owner George Bailey, told the disgruntled townspeople who had stormed the bank, "Your money isn't here… It's in Sam's house… It's in Joe's store." He was explaining the traditional role of the neighborhood bank: to take people's deposits and loan that money to people who will use it to buy and improve their homes, build their businesses and, through countless individual acts, strengthen their communities.

This system of business worked well enough in the 19th century, but by the time of the Great Depression it was fatally overstretched. From the stock market crash of 1929 to the end of 1933, about 9,000 banks had to "suspend operations," and depositors lost about $1.3 billion dollars. The financial system was on the verge of collapse. The country's manufacturing and agricultural sectors, unable to borrow money, were operating at a fraction of capacity.

Protecting American savings

Public outcry led Congress to pass the Bank Act of 1933. Among its many provisions, the Act created the Federal Deposit Insurance Corporation. For the first time, the government now stood behind banks, insuring deposits and restoring confidence to the system. No longer would panicked depositors bring down banks, nor would business grind to a halt as the fear of bank failure brought about contraction in the money supply.

The Federal Deposit Insurance Corporation (FDIC) has

been a tremendous success. Since its creation, there hasn't been a single case of a single depositor losing even one penny of insured deposits in a bank failure. Individual banks have come and gone, but depositors have remained safe. In late 2008, the FDIC temporarily raised the limit on the deposits it insures to $250,000. So conservative investors, intent on preserving rather than growing their assets, could put up to $250,000 in a single bank account, earn interest at prevailing rates, retrieve their money whenever they wanted it and know that it was protected by the full faith and credit of the United States government. If you have more than $250,000 on hand, you simply divide it among insured accounts.

It's not just conservative investors who use banks, either. Banks can be a great place to park money you've earmarked for bigger things. That's why even aggressive investors may choose to hold a portion of their investments in cash, accepting a lower rate of return relative to other investments, in exchange for the ability to have ready access to that cash whenever they need it. A down payment on a house would be an example of such a need.

The Federal Reserve

The Bank Act of 1933 also created the Federal Reserve system, the network of U.S. central banks that sets fiscal and monetary policy and helps keep the national economy on an even keel. The key tool the Fed uses to heat up or cool down the economy is the power to control interest rates.

The basic interest rate—the Federal Funds Rate—is the

rate at which banks lend money to each other on a short-term basis. When the Fed moves to raise or lower its interest rate by, say, a quarter of a percentage point, major commercial banks raise or lower their "prime rate" by a similar amount.

So, by raising interest rates when the economy appears to be overheating and lowering those rates when the economy cools, the Federal Reserve seeks to promote a nice, steady pace of growth. It takes a sensitive hand to keep the monetary policy thermostat set at the proper temperature—keeping inflation low without sending us into a recession. And those interest rates affect us all.

When rates are high, we earn more on our bank deposits and CDs. But higher rates increase the cost of credit for everyone. It costs more to finance our lives. The prices we pay for food, clothing and just about everything else may rise, because higher rates ultimately mean that it costs businesses more to make and ship their products, and they pass those costs along to us.

So do we like it better when interest rates are low? Well, it's easier to get a bigger loan. But money is worth less and demand for goods increases. Inflation starts creeping up. And the cycle begins anew. That's part of what makes it so interesting. There are no hard and fast answers. It's all relative. And that's why you have to consider your investments in the context of the big picture.

$$$ WHAT DID WE LEARN? $$$

1. The world runs on credit.

Without credit, without trust in the ability of borrowers to repay, commerce would grind to a halt.

2. Banks are the primary source of credit.

While there are many non-traditional lenders in the system, banks are by far the largest source of funds for businesses and individuals.

3. The U.S. banking system is considered the safest in the world.

Thanks to FDIC insurance, first instituted during the Great Depression, depositors are generally protected even if banks fail.

4. Interest rates are the Federal Reserve's basic tool in easing or tightening the amount of credit in the financial system.

To keep growth smooth and steady, the Federal Reserve bank lowers and raises interest rates in response to recessionary or inflationary pressures. When rates go up, credit costs rise and demand slows. When rates go down, borrowing money is less expensive and demand increases.

Coming up...

In the next section of this book, I'll point out the common mistakes people make and the financial traps they fall into. And I'll give you the tools you need to make the right choices for your financial future.

3 | PUTTING YOUR HOUSE IN ORDER

"How pleasant it is to have money!"

— Arthur Hugh Clough (1819-1861)

I f you're a NASCAR driver, you can't afford to be leaking fuel on the racetrack. You won't be able to get the power you need. You won't be able to drive as far. You'll have to keep pulling over for more gas while your competitors accelerate around the track. It's the same with debt and your financial future. You can't cruise smoothly to where you want to go if you're "leaking" money.

So before you can build your future, you have to make sure you're not weighed down by the past. You've got to get out of debt, because you need all your resources focused on going forward.

Good debt versus bad debt

Not all debt is bad, however. Most homeowners, for example,

have a mortgage. A mortgage means you can live in your house even though the bank, and not you, owns part of it. A mortgage gives you tax benefits as well. And a mortgage gives you the luxury of not having to pay for your house all at once; so you can take the money you would have had to pay and invest it for a higher rate of return than the rate of interest you're paying on your mortgage.

Say your mortgage costs you $600 a month. Take another $50 a month and save it. That's $600 a year. If you invested that $600 over 30 years—the life of the typical mortgage—at an annual compound rate of 10 percent, you'd have $113,966.27. At the same time, you'd be living in the house and, most likely, watching its value grow over time. So, it's pretty clear that a mortgage is a good kind of debt to have, as long as you can comfortably afford the payments.

At the other end of the spectrum, there's credit card debt. Most of us have credit cards, of course, and many of us carry a balance on them. In fact, in 2008, 75 percent of U.S. households had credit cards—the average adult had nine of them—and 40 percent of those cardholders carry a balance.[4] It seems to be a normal thing to do.

But it's really a bad idea. Credit card debt is extremely expensive. Interest rates range up to 30 percent a year. That means for every $1,000 dollars you carry on your balance, the credit card company could be charging you $300 each year. Three hundred dollars can mean a lot of things—a decent TV, a car payment or new clothes for the kids. Or you could invest that $300, so it would make more money for you. The one thing none of us should do is take that hard-earned money and send it to the credit card companies just for letting us spend more than we can afford.

If I could give you just six words of advice, they'd be "Pay off your credit card debt."

If I could add one more word, it would be "Now."

Saving and investing

How much are you saving? What kind of retirement plan do you have? Do you contribute to an IRA or a 401(k)? Do you understand dollar cost averaging? The power of compounding?

If your answer to any of the above is "huh?" then please read on. And please pay attention.

Regular, consistent, disciplined saving and investing is the best, most foolproof way for you to achieve a higher level of financial security for yourself and your family. I won't say it's the only way—you could always win the lottery or marry rich—but your odds are much better if you build your future step by step.

You'd be amazed at how little it takes to start on the path to living large. The trick is to put money into your future regularly. Invest a bit of every paycheck. Thanks to the power of compound interest, even $1,000 a year—just $20 a week—can grow into a significant amount if given sufficient time.

For more on this and to actually do your own calculation, you can go to www.money.cnn.com/retirement/tools where you'll find a calculator called, "How Fast Will Your Savings Grow?"

Here's how compound interest works: let's say you've got a

$1,000 investment and it earns 10 percent a year. At the end of year one you've got $1,100. At the end of year two, though, you don't have $1,200. You've got $1,210, because you're earning interest on the interest you received in the first year, as well as interest on the original invested amount. Over time the interest you earn on the interest adds up. In ten years, your $1,000 has grown to $2,594. It grows to $4,177 in 15 years; $6,727 in 20. And that's without your contributing even another penny to your original investment.

Someone once wrote something about "the fierce urgency of now." That writer wasn't talking about investing, but he might as well have been. It's never too late to start and there's never been a better moment to begin.

Tax-advantaged savings plans

Do you have a job? If so, good. Does your employer offer an investment plan for retirement? If so, even better. Retirement plans, such as IRAs and 401(k) plans, allow your investments to grow "tax deferred." That means you don't pay income tax on the money you invest, or on the growth of that money while it's in the account. You can keep all the profits you make on your retirement plan assets, and reinvest those profits to get the benefits of compounding, for as long as that money is kept in the plan. And if that's not enough of an incentive, many companies match a percentage of your 401(k) contribution to encourage saving.

You can read more about voluntary defined contribution plans such as 401(k)s, 403(b)s and IRAs at www.money.cnn.

com/retirement/guide/401kandCos.

When you reach retirement age and begin withdrawing your plan assets, you'll have to pay income taxes on the withdrawals, but thanks to the compound returns you've earned, you're still way ahead. The government doesn't give us that many great deals; let's take advantage of the opportunities when they're here.

401(k) plans

Contributing money to a 401(k) gives you an immediate tax deduction, tax-deferred growth on your savings and (usually) a matching contribution from your company. That matching contribution is about as close to a free lunch as there is, so eat up.

Thanks to the Tax Relief Reconciliation Act of 2001, there are a few changes to 401(k)s that may be of even greater benefit to you. For starters, the federal limit on annual contributions is allowed to increase every year until 2011 to keep pace with the cost of living. And, workers 50 and older may now contribute an additional amount—$5,000 as of this writing—above the maximum allowable 401(k) contribution. It's a great way to make up for lost time.

Of course, while federal law sets the guidelines for 401(k) plans, your employer may set tighter restrictions. Plus, it may take time for the administrators of your plan to implement the changes.

For all its tax advantages, the 401(k) is not a penalty-free ride. Pull out money from your account before age 59 and a half, and with few exceptions, you'll owe income taxes on the amount withdrawn plus an additional 10 percent penalty.

Also, be aware of your plan's vesting schedule—that's the time you're required to work at the company before you're allowed to walk away with 100 percent of your employer matches. Of course, any money you contribute to a 401(k) is yours.

Individual Retirement Account (IRA)

An IRA is another excellent long-term option for you. Like a 401(k), IRAs offer huge tax breaks. Even if you have a 401(k) or other tax-advantaged savings plan at work, you should consider investing in an IRA to augment your retirement savings plan.

There are two types of IRAs: a traditional IRA offers tax-deferred growth, meaning you pay taxes on your investment gains only when you make withdrawals and, if you qualify, your contributions may be deductible; and a Roth IRA, by contrast, doesn't allow for deductible contributions (you put money in after you've paid taxes on it), but it offers tax-free growth, meaning you owe no tax when you make withdrawals. With a little study, you can determine which is best for you.

A traditional IRA comes in two "flavors": deductible and nondeductible. You may qualify for a deductible IRA, which lets you deduct all or part of your contributions from your taxable income, if you meet the following guidelines:

- You have no retirement plan at work and you're under 70-1/2. (If you have a non-working spouse, he or she may also invest up to the federal limit and deduct the full amount, so long as your combined earned income as a couple is below the allowable maximum. To check the current allowable maximum, visit www. irs.gov/retirement and click on the "IRA Contribution and Deduction Limits" headline.)

• If you have a 401(k) or other retirement plan at work, you may fully or partially deduct your IRA contribution only if your adjusted gross income (AGI) qualifies. (Again, visit www.irs.gov/retirement and click on the "IRA Contribution and Deduction Limits" headline to see if you qualify.)

• If you're not covered by a retirement plan, but your spouse is, you may qualify for a full or partial deduction if you file jointly and your AGI is below the maximum allowable level. (The same rule applies if you're a non-working spouse of someone covered by a retirement plan at work.) To check the current limit, visit www. irs.gov/retirement and click on the "IRA Contribution and Deduction Limits" headline.

If you're not eligible to contribute to a deductible IRA, you still may be eligible to contribute to a Roth IRA if you're either single or married, filing jointly or singly and your adjusted gross income (AGI) is below the current limit. To check the current limit, visit www.irs.gov/retirement and click on the "IRA Contribution and Deduction Limits" headline.

Note that if you make too much to qualify for a Roth IRA and are not eligible for a deductible IRA, a nondeductible IRA is a valid option. Your contribution won't be deductible, but at least your savings will grow tax-free. As in similar cases, you'll have to pay income tax on your withdrawals.

The other point to stress here is the importance of regular investing. If you put a set amount of money into stocks, or bonds, or mutual funds—and, by the way, I believe that mutual funds, index funds and exchange traded funds (ETFs) are the most appropriate investment choices for the vast majority of the investing public—each month, each pay period or even each week, then you benefit in several ways.

First, of course, you're building both discipline and wealth, and those are both good things. Second, you're giving yourself the opportunity to take advantage of compounding, the best friend you'll ever have. And third, you're using what financial professionals call "dollar cost averaging."

Here's what that's about. If, for example, you're putting the same amount every month into mutual funds, you automatically buy more shares when prices are down and fewer shares when prices are high. They've done research on this, and it turns out that dollar cost averaging reduces your cost per share.

Say you decide to buy $100 worth of ABC each month for three months. In January, the price is $33 a share, so you buy three shares. In February it's $25 and you buy four shares. In March it's down to $20 and you buy five shares. Now you've got 12 shares at an average cost of $25 each. If you'd bought four shares each month regardless of cost, you'd have paid $312—4 percent more—for those same 12 shares.

So, same amount of money invested each month: good. Same amount of shares purchased each month: somewhat less good. Not doing anything each month: bad.

Investing versus inflation

The goal for most of us is simple. We want to become wealthier—able to buy more goods and services than we can buy now—by accumulating assets more quickly than inflation can reduce their value.

If we lived in a static world, investing might be less important. Sure we'd *want* more money, but since the world stayed the same and prices never rose, we wouldn't really *need* more money, assuming we were comfortable with the lives we lived. (We'd still want more, though. For sure.)

But the world we actually live in is more complicated. In real life, standing still is the same as going backward. There's a pernicious, insidious force that eats away at our money like a termite. It's called inflation.

If, for example, Rip Van Winkle had put $100 under his mattress in 1990 and gone to sleep until 2009, he'd awaken to discover that his $100 was still there, untouched. At first he'd feel relieved that no one had taken his money. But he'd soon be horrified at how much less his money bought today than it had in 1990.

When he went downstairs for his first breakfast, Rip would be aghast to discover that the dozen eggs he'd bought for fifty cents in 1990 now cost $3.79. He used to buy a pound of hamburger for a dollar. Today those burgers would cost him $3.29. The cost of a New York City subway ride has doubled. Toilet paper has nearly tripled in price, going from $1.37 to $3.89 a package. The shock of it all might give poor Rip a headache. When he bought himself some aspirin, though, he'd get another one—aspirin has gone from $3.19 to $6.99 a bottle![4]

In effect, in 2008, Rip's $100 bought him only 60 percent of what it bought in 1990. Let's say that instead of putting $100 under his pillow, Rip had invested it in an S&P 500 index fund. He would have received an 8.75 percent annualized rate of return and he would have had $453 when he woke up. Even if you adjust that for inflation, his investment still would have given him $279 worth of buying power. Almost triple what his $100 was worth when he fell asleep. And that's without adding another cent.

What causes inflation? Several things, but basically demand: too many dollars chasing too few goods. It means that today you must pay more for the same amount of the same things you bought last year. And when inflation happens, it affects every part of the economy.

If the price of oil goes up, for example, we can see inflation very clearly when we fill up at the pump. But it also exists in less obvious areas. Food costs more, because it's become more expensive to transport beef or lettuce or cereal across the country. Inflation affects your electric bill, because it costs the power company more money to generate electricity from its gas- and oil-powered equipment. And because petroleum is the raw material in plastic, increased oil prices raise the cost of everything from computer monitors to kitchen utensils.

That's why we need to invest. We have to at least keep pace with inflation if we don't want our standard of living to decline. And we have to earn enough to outpace inflation if we want to improve our lives. Not just for now, but down the road. The future is unknowable, so the more you can do to be prepared for anything, the better off you're likely to be the day that "anything" comes along. Think retirement. Inflation may be relatively stable right now, but it can wake up and come at you like a hungry bear. You need solid investments to make sure you've got enough money to keep living comfortably when you stop working.

$$$ WHAT DID WE LEARN? $$$

1.   There's good debt and bad debt.

Good debt, such as a mortgage, allows us to get the benefit of large, important possessions though we don't yet own them. Bad debt, such as credit card debt, makes us pay extra to live beyond our means.

2.   Smart savers use the power of compounding.

Compounding—earning money on our money—is a powerful wealth creator over time. The earlier you start saving and investing, the greater the effects of compound interest.

3.   Tax-advantaged investing makes sense on every level.

In 401 (k) plans and IRAs, we can invest free of taxes, so our returns grow more quickly. We don't pay taxes on our investments until we withdraw them from the plan.

4.   We must invest to stay ahead of inflation.

Inflation is the rise in prices that eats away at the value of our money. By investing, we can grow our money faster than inflation, so we can to protect and increase our purchasing power.

Coming up...

The next chapters will give you the tools to build your financial house. I'll discuss the principles that professional investors use to increase return, minimize risk and take advantage of opportunities that exist in all market conditions.

I'll show you how to map out an investment strategy that's right for your individual situation: your age, your income level, your family status, your wants and needs. And I'll show you how to modify your investment plan as your needs evolve over time.

Take it from me—you're not the same person at 40 that you were at 20. We all change as we grow, and our investments should, too.

4 | THE WORLD OF INVESTMENTS

"Though mothers and fathers gives us life, it is money alone which preserves it."

— Ihara Saikaku (1642-1693)

Now that you've gotten rid of unwanted debt, learned about the effects of inflation and cleared the decks for action, let's take a look at the investment marketplace. It's a bustling, sprawling universe. Like a shopping mall, it offers the best of the broader world. And, like a mall, it has items for every taste and budget.

There are blue-chip stocks, analogous to high-end retail stores. You know that if you buy one of those stocks, the odds are good that, like fine china or a Tiffany diamond ring, it will increase in value over time. There are medium-term government bonds, like a mid-scale department store, practical, safe, a bit unexciting maybe, but necessary. There are small company stocks and emerging market debt. They're like those kiosks in the middle of the mall, the ones selling the little trinkets that look good but whose quality is unknown. Still, they're priced so attractively it might be worth taking a chance. You could uncover a real gem in the midst of the cut-glass baubles.

Let's focus on the major categories:
- stocks
- bonds
- cash equivalents
- international stocks
- commodities

By understanding each of them—what they are and how they behave—you'll be better able to determine how they might fit in your own investment portfolio.

Stocks

When you buy a stock, you are buying a share of a company. You are a part owner. You suffer through the vagaries of its performance in exchange for a portion of the profits. A great many factors affect a company's profitability: the state of the overall economy, the company's position versus its competitors, its labor situation, its cost of supplies, distribution and advertising, its management team, its financial controls, the legal and regulatory environment—the list goes on and on.

Some people buy stocks for appreciation; some for income. Income, when it comes from bonds, is from the interest or coupon. In stocks, income comes from dividends—a portion of the profit paid to investors in proportion to the number of shares they hold. Like a bond yield, a company's dividend is stated as an actual amount of money per share (for example, on September 22, 2008, General Electric announced a quarterly dividend of $0.31 per share), not a percentage of the stock price. That means when dividend-paying stocks go down in price, the dividend, as a percentage of the price, increases. Income from dividends can be re-invested to buy more stock, or you can use that income, which is paid quarterly, for anything you want.

As the company prospers, its dividend payments increase and shareholders prosper as well. Some companies are known for paying high dividends relative to other companies in the same category. Even if the stock price of these companies does not appreciate as quickly as the stock price of some others, investors still do well thanks to predictable, generous dividend payments. With a sufficient number of shares, the dividend payments can be useful income. Or, if not spent, the dividends can be re-invested in shares of the company. Remember our talk about compounding? It works with dividends, too.

Of course, if a company does poorly it may cut its dividend or skip paying it altogether. Even in bad times, though, companies are loath to cut or suspend dividends, because many people take it as a sign of deep trouble and sell their shares, driving down the value of the company overall.

If there are troubles and if the company ultimately goes bankrupt, you, as an investor, are not well protected. You could lose the entire value of your investment in the firm.

But let's look at the positive side. The second way investors profit is from appreciation in the value of the shares themselves. The stock price of a company can rise for a great number of reasons: the overall economy is growing and bringing the company along with it; the sector in which the company operates (energy, pharmaceuticals, retail, transportation, etc.) is experiencing a boom; the company has a new product or process that gives it a competitive advantage in the marketplace; the company is well positioned to take advantage of seasonal, demographic or climate-related conditions, etc. The constant in all of these examples is the expectation of increased profitability ahead. In other words, the stock price reflects the public's confidence—or lack of it—in greater earnings going forward.

Stocks are highly liquid. They are traded daily on exchanges all over the world, and investors can buy and sell at any time. Also, the workings of the companies that issue stock are a matter of public record. By law, these companies must file quarterly financial statements with government agencies, must open their books to auditors and must comply with federal regulations designed to protect the investing public. There are a number of agencies involved in overseeing the fair and honest conduct of market activity; the Securities and Exchange Commission (SEC) is the federal agency with the greatest responsibility—and the greatest power—to enforce standards (unless a crime is committed, in which case the Department of Justice and the FBI step in).

There have certainly been some "bad apples" over the years. In a huge scandal in 2001, Enron Corporation defrauded investors and then went bankrupt. In 2002, the same thing happened at WorldCom. But by and large, the U.S. stock market is transparent and behaves according to standard, recognized rules.

Companies are valued in two basic ways: market value and enterprise value. To get the enterprise value—the total worth of the company—you'd subtract the company's debt from its market value.

To assess the market value of a company, you can multiply its stock price by the number of its shares. For example, on October 1, 2007, General Electric, one of the largest and most stable companies in the world, had 9.96 billion shares. They traded at a price of $42.02 per share. The company was worth $419 billion. A year later, on October 1, 2008, those same 9.96 billion shares were trading at $24.50 each. The company was now worth $244 billion, less than 60 percent of its former value. The company still had the same products, same factories, same management talent and the same employees. But investor sentiment had changed. The overall economy was in free-fall and near-term sales prospects looked dismal.

So it's easy to see that the key determinant of an individual company's stock price is the market's view of that company's near-term earnings. If the market expects the company to do well, the stock rises. If the market expects the company to stumble—for reasons that can range from a declining national economy to problems within the company itself—then the stock price falls.

The ratio of the price of a company's stock to its yearly earnings per share is a handy—but not foolproof—assessment of whether or not a stock is valued appropriately. The ratio is called, not surprisingly, the price-to-earnings, or P/E ratio. A high ratio means investors are paying more for each unit of return. A low ratio may be a signal that the stock is undervalued—or it could be a sign that the market believes the company has troubles.

Over time, "normal" P/E ratios have been established for different sectors in the market. If we look at General Electric again, the company's earnings per share for the year ended September 30, 2007 were $2.14. If we divide that day's GE stock price by the earnings per share, we get a ratio of 19.64. That's a reasonable ratio, by historical standards, for a large conglomerate. The stock was not necessarily a bargain at that price, but it was not a rip-off either.

For the year ended September 30, 2008, earnings per share were $2.11. Dividing $2.11 into that day's stock price gives a ratio of 11.61. By historical standards, the company's stock was substantially undervalued—in other words, cheap—on that date. Viewed rationally, it could be considered a buying opportunity. But the market is a herd animal, and in October 2008 it was stampeding toward the exits.

Bonds

Whether you buy a municipal bond, a savings bond or a corporate bond, the underlying premise is the same. A bond is a loan. You are not buying a piece of a company; you are loaning money to an entity (corporate or government) for a defined period of time at a fixed interest rate.

These entities—companies, municipalities, states and U.S. and foreign governments—use bonds to finance many different kinds of projects and activities. In return for your money, the issuer promises to pay you a fixed amount every year for the life of the bond, and to return the entire amount of your loan at the end of the time period.

It's straightforward: the bond itself will state the interest rate (coupon) that will be paid, and state when the loaned funds (bond principal) are to be returned (maturity date). Interest on bonds is usually paid every six months. The main categories of bonds are corporate bonds, municipal bonds and U.S. Treasury bonds, notes and bills, which are collectively referred to as "Treasuries."

Two features of a bond—credit quality and time to maturity—are the main determinants of a bond's interest rate. Bond maturities range from a 90-day Treasury bill to a 30-year government bond. Corporate and municipals are typically in the 3- to 10-year range.

Bonds are referred to as "fixed income" investments, because you know in advance what your return will be. The income is "fixed." In that sense, a bond is a very safe investment. You know what you will get. That's why bonds are often good for people on fixed budgets who can't afford not to receive a known quantity of money every year.

You can also sell the bonds you buy. Perhaps you decide that the return you are earning, while decent, is less than you believe you could get in the stock market. The bond market is highly liquid, you can sell your bond easily.

By the same token, you don't have to buy bonds from the issuer alone. Let's say that five years ago, the government issued a 10-year bond paying 7 percent interest. Today, with a stock market on the rocks and low inflation, a 7 percent coupon might look pretty good. You can purchase a pre-owned bond from someone who, for whatever reason, is willing to sell it.

But if, due to market conditions, the bond is more attractive now than it was when it was issued, you will have to pay more than its face value to obtain that guaranteed 7 percent coupon per year. If it was a $100 bond at issuance, for example, you might have to pay $110 for it. Conversely, if the market for bonds has weakened, you might be able to pick it up for $90.

The relationship of price to yield

There's more to the story, though. If prevailing interest rates—those not connected to your bond—decline, from 5 percent to 3 percent for example, your 7 percent coupon is more valuable, because it represents a guaranteed, virtually risk-free rate of return that is significantly higher than an investor could get from a savings account, money market mutual fund or CD.

If, conversely, interest rates rise to 8 or 9 percent, then the bond will be worth less and its market price will reflect this fact.

If you buy a 10-year $100 bond at par—the price at which it was issued—and it pays an annual return of 7 percent, then you have an actual return—a current yield, it's called—of 7 percent. But if prevailing interest rates rise, the price of the bond will decline. Let's say you buy it at $90. The 7 percent coupon the bond pays on its $100 face value remains fixed. But the current yield—the actual percentage return on your investment—is greater than 7 percent. That's because the $7 interest you earn each year (7 percent of $100) is 8 percent of the $90 you paid for the bond.

The term "coupon" comes from the way bonds were originally marketed: investors received a coupon book and twice a year they were entitled to rip a coupon from the book and redeem it for the promised interest payment.

While the coupon rate does not vary, the bond itself becomes more or less valuable over time as overall interest rates change. It doesn't affect you if you bought the bond when it was first issued and you plan to hold it until maturity. If that's the case, the changes in the bond's value mean zip.

But for those trading in bonds, those fluctuations are profit opportunities. It's like a see-saw: when the price rises, yield declines. In other words, when prevailing interest rates rise, the bond is worth less but the fixed percentage coupon is worth more relative to the bond's cost. When interest rates fall, the bond itself is worth more but its coupon is worth less as a percentage. We can summarize the situation this way: price up; yield down. Price down; yield up.

Bonds have at least two kinds of risk. One is that the interest rate the bond is paying will be lower than the current prevailing interest rate or, worse yet, lower than the rate of inflation. Should that occur—and historically it has—your bonds will be worth less, because the money is worth less. If you don't sell, though, you earn the promised interest rate throughout the life of the bond and you're paid 100 percent of the principal upon maturity.

Another kind of risk is that the corporation, municipality or other entity issuing the bond will go out of business, lose all its money, be wiped off the face of the Earth or in some other way default on its obligation to you. This is the most serious risk of all.

Of course, there are rating agencies whose entire mission is to assess the strength of bond issuers. These organizations, such as Moody's, Standard & Poor and Fitch Ratings, examine the financial health of the issuers and give them a letter grade: AAA is the highest, next comes AA+, AA, AA-, A+, etc., down to the letter B. In the murky waters below B are "high-yield" bonds, also called "junk bonds."

A bond's assigned rating is directly related to the strength of the issuer and the risk that the issuer will default on its payments. It's the same reason a sub-prime mortgage holder pays higher interest—sub-prime represents a bigger risk for the bank.

For example, junk bonds pay the highest rate of interest because they have the greatest risk of default. If they didn't pay so well, no one would invest in them. But at a high enough rate of return, there will be some investors willing to take the risk in order to reap the potential rewards.

Conversely, the more highly rated the institution, the more certain the repayment and the lower the interest rate the bonds will offer. Remember, risk and return go together. Not just between asset classes but within them as well.

As we've noted, bonds come in different maturities as well, from 90 days to 30 years. The longer the time to maturity, the greater is the risk of inflation eating away at the value of returns. To compensate, long-term bonds generally pay higher rates of interest than shorter-term instruments.

Certain kinds of bonds also allow you to collect your interest free of taxes. Municipal bonds, issued by states, counties and cities to fund public works projects, are typical examples. The interest they pay is generally free of federal taxes and, for in-state residents, the bonds are free of state and local taxes too. They're good vehicles for individuals in high tax brackets. For many of these people, a five-and-a-half percent non-taxable return is better than an 8 percent taxable one, because the government would take up to 40 percent of the return in taxes.

In addition to shopping for bonds issued by the U.S. government, government agencies, states, municipalities, utilities, authorities and corporations, investors also have access to international opportunities.

The Kingdom of Saudi Arabia may issue a 20-year bond to pay for the development of a huge gas field so far from any settled territory that it will require the construction of a new city just to house the workers who will ultimately drill there. The Chinese Development Corporation, a partnership between the Chinese government and private investors, might issue a bond to pay for the construction of a new toll road. Greater tax revenue resulting from the increased economic activity along the road, and tolls from the road itself, will help the project pay for itself over time. The Argentine government might float a 15-year bond to cover the cost of building a dam and hydroelectric plant in Patagonia. You get the picture—there are lots of bonds with different levels of risk and return.

Cash equivalents

Cash equivalents are highly liquid, very safe investments that can be easily converted into cash, such as Treasury Bills and money market funds. These investments generally earn a low rate of interest because of the certainty of return.

The most common examples of cash equivalents are:
- Savings deposits
- Certificates of Deposit (CDs)
- Money market deposit accounts
- Money market mutual funds

When you deposit your money, you're actually lending it to a financial institution. The institution, in turn, lends your money to businesses and to government agencies. The institution earns interest on the loans and then pays some or all of that interest to you. Generally, savings vehicles are very safe. With the exception of CDs, which have pre-determined time parameters, when you want your money back, you can withdraw it quickly and without penalty.

Even though cash equivalents don't earn a great deal of interest, they are still appropriate for a portion of many investors' money. Savers buy cash equivalents so they can put their money in a safe place and access it quickly. Investors buy cash equivalents as a temporary "parking place" for their money while they're deciding what new investments to make.

The FDIC, a federal government agency, insures savings deposits, CDs and money market deposit accounts for up to $250,000 per account per institution. Generally speaking, money market mutual funds are not FDIC insured, but most have Securities Investor Protection Corporation (SIPC) coverage, a private insurance program for mutual fund companies and brokerage firms. For these reasons, cash equivalents tend to have considerably less capital risk than stocks or bonds.

For those who prefer credit unions to banks, the National Credit Union Administration (NCUA), a federal agency, charters and supervises federal credit unions. The NCUA also insures savings in federal and most state-chartered credit unions, up to the same limits as the FDIC, through the National Credit Union Share Insurance Fund, a federal fund backed by the full faith and credit of the United States government.

The most significant risk to cash equivalents is inflation. If inflation occurs at a rate higher than the rate you're earning from your cash equivalents, your money loses its purchasing power. For example, if you earn 1 percent from a savings account and inflation is running at 3 percent, your money isn't keeping up with the rising cost of goods and services. One hundred dollars in your savings account will grow to $101 by the end of the year, but a dress that costs $100 today will increase in price to $103 over the same time period.

By the way, just because something "feels" like a cash equivalent doesn't mean it is; and a low return doesn't guarantee that something *is* a cash equivalent.

International stocks and bonds

In today's world, no one market, region or country consistently outperforms all the others. While the U.S. is still the world's largest economy, Europe and Japan—the other developed markets—offer opportunities as well. And you'll often hear talk of BRIC (Brazil, Russia, India and China) and other emerging market nations, taking their place on the international investment stage.

Broadening your investment horizon to include international stocks increases your chances of finding true bargains. After all, although the United States is one of the most innovative nations in the world, it's not the only one. New products, new ideas and new technologies are being discovered and developed all around the world.

In addition, as free trade booms, the world becomes a smaller place. New consumer markets have opened, increasing demand for cellphones and computers, automobiles, homes and all kinds of consumer goods and services. Banks, retailers, cement companies and even life insurance companies have sprung up all around the planet, and their hungry consumers allow them to grow much faster than their U.S. counterparts.

It might surprise you to learn that 11 of the world's 20 largest companies are headquartered outside the United States.[5] They may do a significant portion of their business here, but home is on another shore. According to *Forbes* magazine, the largest construction, auto, business equipment and food companies are all non-U.S. firms.

Until the early years of this century, information on day-to-day non-U.S. stock prices was difficult to obtain, and it was nearly impossible to access accurate corporate financial information. But the Internet really has opened the world to almost anyone, and now you can obtain precise information from Hong Kong, Japan, Russia, Brazil or any of the world's exchanges and markets with just a few clicks of a mouse. Reliable data makes these markets knowable and, as a result, you can buy and sell investments from those countries with a much higher degree of confidence.

Part of the reason for the strong performance of non-U.S. stocks is that money has been pouring into international investments. It's not that money is necessarily running away from the U.S., it's just flowing to other places much more quickly.

According to the Investment Company Institute, there is now almost as much money in international stock funds as there is in U.S.-only funds. In fact, non-U.S. funds outsold domestic U.S. investment mutual funds by almost 4 to 1 between 2003 and 2006.

There's a case to be made, too, that if you're building a diversified portfolio, you should include international stocks and bonds in proportion to their weight in the global marketplace. These investments help your portfolio reflect the world as it is and they help to protect you from over-concentration in one region.

Most financial advisers today would suggest that you should have some exposure to non-U.S. assets. In today's smaller, more accessible world, it makes sense for you to follow opportunity wherever it is.

Commodities

Commodities are tangible assets, raw materials useful in and of themselves or as ingredients in manufactured products. They include oil, gasoline, livestock, precious metals, sugar, timber and more. Commodities are a distinct asset class with returns that are largely independent of stock and bond returns. Adding commodities to a portfolio of stocks and bonds can, therefore, provide diversification benefits, helping to lower your risk and boost your potential return. And, because they're traded and used globally, they can provide you with international exposure as well.

It's only recently that investing in commodities became possible for the average investor. After all, you don't really want to own the physical commodity itself: there's no benefit in having a herd of cattle delivered to your doorstep. But in the past decade, we've seen the introduction of products that allow you to invest in a broad range of commodities.

Commodities have always been seen as a hedge against inflation because, historically, their prices have risen faster than inflation has. When times are flush and demand puts upward pressure on the price of goods and services, then the price of the commodities used in those goods and services rises even more quickly. When people don't buy as much—in a recession, say—then the price of commodities tends to decline along with the economy.

As we've noted, the performance of commodities is not closely correlated to that of stocks and bonds, so commodities can provide excellent diversification within a portfolio. By contrast, stocks—whether individually or in mutual funds —often have a positive correlation to one another and cannot offer the same diversification benefits. In other words, you may own a very diverse group of stocks, but they're unlikely to give you the portfolio diversification you can get from mixing in some commodities.

You don't have to buy individual commodities, either. You can gain exposure to gold, for example, in several different ways: gold bullion, gold coins, stocks of gold mining companies, mutual funds of gold mining stocks and gold ETFs (we'll explain more about funds in chapter 7).

Commodities simply don't behave the same way at the same time as other asset classes.

$$$ WHAT DID WE LEARN? $$$

I. Stocks let you own part of a company.

When you own a share of a company, you participate directly in that company's success.

2. Bonds provide steady, predictable returns if you hold them to maturity.

A bond is a loan you make to a company or government entity for a set period of time at a pre-determined rate of interest.

3. Government insured cash equivalents are the safest investment, but provide the lowest return.

Cash equivalents give you a safe place to put money while you decide how to deploy it more effectively. Over the long term, however, cash equivalents can expose you to inflation risk.

4.   You should consider international stocks and bonds for a portion of your investments.

In a global economy, international stocks and bonds can offer attractive returns and access to opportunities and growth rates not found in the U.S.

5.   Commodities can help protect against inflation.

When prices rise, the prices of commodities tend to rise faster, making them an effective hedge in inflationary times.

Coming up...

Now that we've examined the basic building blocks of the investment universe, let's look at the physics of how these elements behave. Don't worry, I'm not going to go all Copernicus on you. But I want to take you through the principles that can help you build and maintain a hard-working, efficient, growth-producing investment portfolio.

5 | THE KEY PRINCIPLES OF INVESTMENT SUCCESS

"Money begets money."

— John Ray (1627-1705)

You wouldn't build a house without a blueprint (not if you expected it to stay up). And you wouldn't take a cross-country road trip without a map. Anything worth doing is worth planning. Your financial future is no exception.

No matter how smart you are, you couldn't possibly expect to succeed at a game you'd never played unless you at least knew the rules. You'd want to know the strategies. You'd want to understand the tools. You'd want to see how the little moves add up to the big picture.

It's the same with investing. There are certain principles that determine investment performance. They describe the way that different market elements interact with one another, the way they work together over time. Understand them, and you're on the way to success.

These principles can help you construct your portfolio, make your decisions and measure your investment performance against objective standards.

The first thing to know is that, historically, markets rise over time. Markets move in cycles: they go up, they go down, and they go up again. Picture a mountain peak, a valley and then another mountain peak—that's a market cycle. At the end, the new peak is higher than the last one. So even when we're in a deep trough—a recession—we should have faith in the market's ultimate recovery. Because that's what the market has done over and over and over again.

As I write this book, the market is down quite a bit from the all-time high it reached in 2007. Am I worried about the money I invested? Not really. I've made a long-term commitment to my investment plan. Despite the current turbulence, I haven't changed it one bit. I know that the market will recover and that my investments will grow.

That's not to say I enjoy seeing markets fall—I don't. But I recognize that there are good times and bad times. Our country, our world, isn't going away. The energy of the six billion people on our planet will propel us forward. If you stand back far enough and look at market results for the past 80 years, you'd see an almost unbroken line of progress. It's the short term that gives people the jitters.

But the cure for fear is knowledge. So one of my goals is to help you understand the principles that describe how the markets behave.

Principle 1: There is a direct relationship between risk and return.

The most basic rule of investing is this: risk and reward go together. The asset classes with the best long-term performance also have the greatest year-to-year fluctuation in value.

That fluctuation, called "volatility," is what makes certain asset classes risky: in the short term you never know what you're going to get.

Let's look at the three major categories of investments: stocks, bonds and cash equivalents. Assume you'd placed $1,000 in each of these three categories 30 years ago. How much would your investment be worth today?

Stocks, Bonds, Bills and Inflation

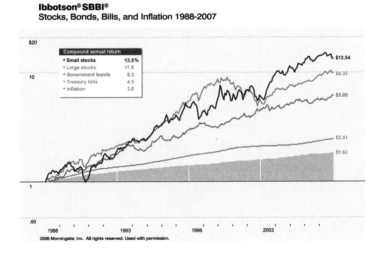

Ibbotson® SBBI®
Stocks, Bonds, Bills, and Inflation 1988-2007

Compound annual return	
• Small stocks	13.5%
• Large stocks	11.8
• Government bonds	9.3
• Treasury bills	4.5
• Inflation	3.0

$12.54
$9.33
$5.89
$2.41
$1.82

1988   1993   1998   2003

It's not even close! You can see that the performance of large and small stocks leaves bonds and cash in the dust. Over the long term, despite the occasional blips and hiccups, stocks have clearly bested all other asset categories.

But looking year to year, it's a different story.

Year-Over-Year Fluctuations in Returns

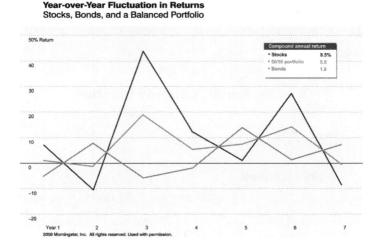

Year-over-Year Fluctuation in Returns
Stocks, Bonds, and a Balanced Portfolio

Viewed in the short term, you can see that stocks are very volatile—if you need your money in a hurry, there's no guarantee you'll have as much as you invested. You could lose money if you have to take it out of the market when the market is down.

Over time, the market pays you a premium for accepting a higher degree of uncertainty about how your investment will perform in any given year. It says, in effect, "Stick with me, kid;

I won't let you down." And with the right time frame, it never has.

About now, you're probably wondering, "What's a typical return for a typical year?" You may also be asking yourself, "What about those bad years? How much can I lose?" Both are good, smart questions.

Let's focus on U.S. large company stocks, one of the major asset classes. Large companies are typically defined as those with capitalization—"worth"—of 10 billion dollars and up. These are the so-called "blue chip" stocks. They're generally among the best known, longest-lived and most stable performers in the stock market. Conversely, small capitalization stocks—shares of newer companies usually valued at under $2 billion, tend to be the least predictable ones. (There are also mid-cap stocks, which fall between large and small. To keep things simple, though, we'll leave them until later.)

You can understand the dichotomy between large- and small-cap stocks by considering the difference between an ocean liner and a speedboat. The speedboat can accelerate quickly, zoom through calm seas and turn on a dime to follow opportunities—a school of fish, say. It can be a thrilling ride. But when conditions change and seas turn rough, the little speedboat is in trouble. Hold onto your stomach. Without sufficient heft to plow through the weather, the boat might not make it.

The ocean liner, by contrast, proceeds in a stately manner through all kinds of conditions. It doesn't go as fast as the speedboat and it doesn't turn as quickly. In very rough seas, passengers may notice some rolling motion. But the ship is large and strong enough to reach its destination regardless of the weather and chances are it will deliver a first-class experience to its passengers along the way.

Within the universe of stocks, then, shares of large companies—we'll call them "large-cap stocks"—are the most predictable performers. Over the 81 years from 1926 to 2007, they have produced an average total return of 10.4 percent. (Total return is the stock price appreciation plus the reinvestment of all the dividends over a given time period.)

That sounds pretty good, but it doesn't tell the whole story. Because the ride to that 10.4 percent average can be mighty bumpy. In the best single year ever for large-cap stocks, they returned 54 percent.[6] But in the worst year ever (before 2008), they lost 43 percent of their value.[7] Ouch! That's volatile.

Volatility is often the most common shorthand for risk. If you're invested in a major stock, risk isn't so much that the company will disappear. It's that you can't predict how much you'll make in any given year.

The concept of volatility is an extremely important one, so please forgive me if I seem to harp on it. The fear of market volatility can make it difficult to plan, to budget and to act.

So how can you determine how volatile your investment will be? Investment professionals use a risk measurement called a standard deviation to figure it out.

Standard deviation: a yardstick for measuring risk

Don't worry; this isn't a math lesson. A standard deviation is a number that indicates how far from its historical average performance your investment is likely to stray in a given year.

So, when the gurus say that large-cap stocks have an annual average return of 10 percent with a 20 percent "risk," it means that most of the time—two-thirds of the time, actually, or four years out of six—you'll earn somewhere between 30 percent on the high side and minus ten percent on the low end of the scale. You'll be plus or minus 20 percent from 10 percent.

In the case of large-cap stocks, then, 20 percent on either side of the average return is one standard deviation. Deviation from what? Deviation from the norm, the average.

Now, what about the other two years out of six? Well, in those years your returns are likely to fall within *two* standard deviations of the norm. In other words, you'll probably be within 40 percentage points of 10 percent on both the upside and the downside. That's a big range, of course—minus 30 percent to plus 50 percent—but we've seen those returns before, and there's no reason to believe we won't see them in the future.

There are even those outlier years that defy the best predictions of the smartest professionals in the business. In those highly unusual years, your $100 investment could grow to more than $150 if you're lucky. Or that same investment could shrink to $50.

Every asset class, from large-cap stocks to government bonds to international stocks, has its own average risk and return coordinates. We can plot them on a graph, making "return" the y-axis (the vertical line) and "risk" the x-axis (the horizontal line).

Let's take a look.

Risk Versus Return

Risk Versus Return
Stocks, Bonds, and Bills 1926-2007

2008 Morningstar, Inc. All rights reserved. Used with permission.

There, that's clearer. Here you can see the risk and return characteristics of five major asset classes: U.S. large-cap stocks, U.S. small-cap stocks, long-term bonds, intermediate-term bonds and cash equivalents.

One glance shows you how it works. The higher the return, the greater the risk. The less certain the earnings in any given year, the greater your earnings over the long term.

And if you're thinking that the lower return doesn't look so bad, given the safety of the investment, take a look at those returns once we've factored in the effects of inflation over time.

Inflation Risk

Inflation Risk: Stocks Versus Fixed Income
Range of average inflation-adjusted returns over 20-year periods 1926-2007

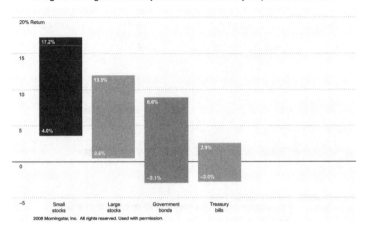

You can see that inflation knocks down the purchasing power of those returns quite a bit. In fact, if you were counting on bonds or treasuries to protect your future, you could find yourself under water just when you were counting on a safe, dry retirement.

So let me ask you a question: when will you need to take your money from the market and start using it? If it's next year, you'll have to think twice about stocks, because who knows what they'll be worth in such a short time frame. You'd have a better chance of earning a positive return in bonds, and you'd have the best chance in cash.

But if you have 5 or 7 or 10 years, or even longer to wait, then it's a different story.

Let's look at our next principle of investing:

Principle 2: Time is your friend.

Historically, time smoothes out volatility. So the longer you stay in the market, the more likely you are to see your investment do what it should.

Let's take a look at how the range of returns narrows when we hold our investments for a longer period of time.

Reduction of Risk Over Time

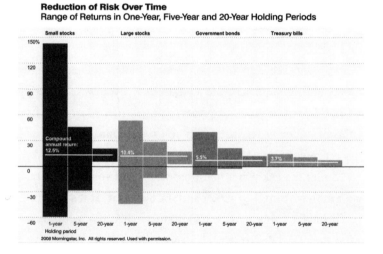

Reduction of Risk Over Time
Range of Returns in One-Year, Five-Year and 20-Year Holding Periods

You can see that even the most volatile asset class, small company stocks, becomes relatively stable when you take the long view. So if you have a reasonable time horizon, you have an excellent chance of high average returns over many years.

And that translates into a comfortable retirement with plenty of cushioning along the way.

YOUR THREE KEY STEPS:

1. Diversify
2. Allocate
3. Optimize

But what if you don't have such a long time horizon? What if you're approaching retirement? What if you're already in retirement? How can you get the returns you want while minimizing the volatility you don't want? I'll give you the answer in one word: diversify.

Principle 3: Diversification lowers your risk and improves your return.

In simplest terms, diversification is the investment version of the saying, "Don't put all your eggs in one basket." A diversified portfolio spreads your investment among multiple asset classes so you're protected from downturns in any one area.

See, although markets move in cycles, individual asset classes generally don't move in the same direction at the same time. So by blending different classes in your portfolio, you can earn steadier returns.

To get the benefits of diversification, you want assets that aren't closely correlated to one another. "Correlation" is a measure of how similarly two asset classes perform. If they're too similar—if they go up and down more or less in tandem— you're not getting much diversification out of owning both of them. On the other hand, if every time one goes up the other goes down, then you've got great diversification.

In the next table, you can see how different asset classes correlate to one another. All correlations are set between 1.00 and -1.00. A correlation of 1.00 means an asset class moves the same amount in the *same* direction at the same time as another. A correlation of -1.00 means an asset class moves the same amount in the *opposite* direction at the same time as another. In real life, asset classes achieve a perfect 1.00 correlation only to themselves; and there are no asset classes that exhibit a perfect -1.00 correlation.

Correlation

Correlation Can Help Evaluate Potential Diversification Benefits
Asset class correlation 1926-2007

	Small stocks	Large stocks	LT corporate bonds	LT govt bonds	IT govt bonds	Treasury bills
Small stocks	1.00					
Large stocks	0.79	1.00				
LT corporate bonds	0.08	0.19	1.00			
LT govt bonds	–0.02	0.12	0.93	1.00		
IT govt bonds	–0.07	0.04	0.89	0.90	1.00	
Treasury bills	–0.10	–0.02	0.20	0.23	0.48	1.00

Maybe you're thinking, "OK, I get it, I sacrifice a little top end in order to have a more stable portfolio." But it's better than that. Diversification doesn't just lower volatility; it can actually improve your earnings.

It's synergy: the different asset classes enhance one another, balancing each other while they smooth your progress toward your goals.

Think of a basketball team: five players, each with different skills. You've got your big guy (or woman) at center, grabbing rebounds. Your point guard dishes the ball to the teammate with the open shot. The power forward can mix it up in the paint, keeping the opponent off balance. Your small forward is a pure shooter with a sweet stroke from outside. Then you've got your small, quick guard, the one who can break down a defense, create turnovers and hang in mid-air forever while soaring to the basket.

It's a great mix, because each one has something the others don't. They complement each other; they don't replicate each other. And if one has an off night, the others will pick up the slack. That, if you will, is non-correlated diversification.

So, how should *you* diversify? Well, the science of constructing a portfolio—determining how much to put into cash, bonds and stocks—is called "asset allocation."

The difference between seat-of-the-pants diversification and careful asset allocation is the difference between a good pick-up basketball team and an NBA franchise. They both play the same basic game, but one of them operates at a substantially higher level.

Asset allocation: the key to results

According to something called "modern portfolio theory," the way you combine your assets is the key to how much you earn.

It's way more important than what you buy or when you buy and sell it. So it's not necessary to chase the hot stock tip or the "brilliant" money manager. You don't have to spend energy trying to figure out the best time to buy or sell. It's more productive to construct a portfolio with the blend of assets that's right for your individual situation.

Those who ignore asset allocation do so at their peril. Asset allocation is *so* important that some experts believe it's responsible for over 90 percent of the difference in performance between one portfolio and another.

The beauty of the theory is that it makes investing easier. The most important thing isn't whether you choose between Home Depot and Lowe's, it's that you have a portfolio that contains stocks, bonds and other investments; it's the blend of asset classes that counts. Just get in it and you'll win it.

Asset Allocation

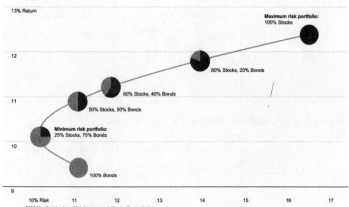

How Asset Allocation Influences Risk and Return
1970-2007

2008 Morningstar, Inc. All rights reserved. Used with permission.

In the previous chart, you can see that adding stocks to a bond portfolio increases return and lowers risk. In fact, a portfolio divided equally between stocks and bonds has approximately the same risk as an all-bond portfolio and provides substantially more return.

Now that you see how diversification can bring more consistency to portfolio performance, and you understand how asset allocation works to improve your returns, it's time for the last big concept: portfolio optimization.

By carefully combining different asset classes, you can "optimize" your portfolio, fine-tuning your financial engine so it delivers every ounce of growth without increasing risk.

Optimization

When the portfolio incurs the least amount of risk for the return you seek, we say it's on the "efficient frontier." It's been tweaked to the max. To continue our basketball analogy, a portfolio on the efficient frontier is an NBA team with all-stars at every position, playing its heart out for a coach who directs the team in such a way that it's even greater than the sum of its stellar parts.

The efficient frontier is a very impressive concept. In fact, in 1990, a Nobel Prize in Economics was awarded to Harry Markowitz, the man who proposed its existence. Markowitz realized that he could construct a portfolio in which each asset class would offset the risk inherent in another. With enough asset classes and enough tinkering, he could tailor a portfolio to deliver the maximum expected return for each unit of risk an investor chose to accept.

The efficient frontier works like this:

Consider a one-year period of time, starting today. As of right now, we know the price of each stock, every bond, etc. What we don't know is what they'll be worth at the end of our one-year time frame.

But based on historical observation, we can make some informed guesses. We can assign an expected return and volatility to each asset class in our portfolio, and we can estimate the correlation of each class to the others. And by knowing these measurements for each of our portfolio components, we can calculate the risk and return of the portfolio as a whole.

Let's say we want a return of 10 percent per year. Well, we can create hundreds of asset combinations that can be expected to earn that 10 percent. They'll all have different risk levels. The "optimal" portfolio is the one that gives you 10 percent with the lowest volatility.

In theory, there are an infinite number of points on the efficient frontier. For any return you expect to receive, there will be a portfolio that can deliver it at the lowest possible level of risk. For any level of risk you're prepared to take, there will be a highest possible expected return. Still, the higher the return, the higher the risk. That's just life.

Very few investors have the time, the tools or the know-how to perform the analysis required to optimize their own portfolios. But any portfolio, except those that are already optimal, can be made more efficient through careful, disciplined asset allocation. This is an area where a professional advisor—a good one—can add value.

$$$ WHAT DID WE LEARN? $$$

1. Risk and return go together.

We learned that it's necessary to accept some risk if we want to beat inflation and build wealth. We also learned that each asset class has its own risk and reward characteristics.

2. Time is your friend.

We saw that time smoothes the effects of volatility, allowing each asset class to produce its expected long-term returns.

3. Diversification can help provide more predictable returns.

We saw that, because asset classes don't all move in lockstep, diversification lowers portfolio risk overall. When stocks are down, for example, bonds may be up. So a portfolio with both stocks and bonds produces more consistent earnings than either asset alone.

4. Asset allocation is your most important portfolio decision.

We learned that asset allocation—the process of dividing your investment among many different kinds of assets—is the key to performance. As we noted, some studies suggest that asset allocation is responsible for more than 90 percent of the difference in returns between portfolios. It's far more important than individual stock or bond selection and market timing combined.

5. You can optimize your portfolio to get the lowest risk for the return you want.

We examined the efficient frontier, that hypothetical curve that gives you the return you want for the least possible risk.

Coming up...

Good job. The concepts we've covered are important, and not always easy to grasp. Thanks for hanging in while I explained them.

And now that you understand the principles of investing, let's put them to work for you.

6 | INSTANT DIVERSIFICATION: MUTUAL FUNDS, INDEX FUNDS & EXCHANGE TRADED FUNDS

"Money speaks sense in a language all nations understand."

— Aphra Behn (1640-1689)

You've probably heard so much about mutual funds that even if you don't own any, it's likely that you know what they are and how they work. But just to clear up any misconceptions and to make sure we're all starting on the same page, let's quickly go over a few of the basics.

A mutual fund pools money from hundreds and thousands of investors to construct a portfolio of stocks, bonds, real estate, or other securities, according to its charter. Each investor in the fund gets a slice of the total pie. One unit of the mutual fund provides a piece of every holding within the fund. Whereas $100 might get you 10 shares of a particular stock, $100 invested in a stock mutual fund will give you a smaller share in the 20 or more stocks that the fund invests in.

In this way, a mutual fund provides ready-made diversification for each dollar invested. Most funds require only moderate minimum investments, from a few hundred to a few thousand dollars, so you can construct a diversified portfolio much more cheaply than you could on your own.

There are a dizzying number of mutual funds in every conceivable asset class: stocks, bonds, money markets, commodities, real estate and more.

In stocks alone, there are growth funds, which buy shares of expanding companies; sector funds, which buy shares of companies in a particular sector, such as technology or health care; and index funds, which buy shares of every stock in a particular index, such as the S&P 500.

That's also the case with bond funds. They exist in every segment of the bond market. If you want safe investments, consider government bond funds; if you're willing to gamble on high-risk investments, try high-yield bond funds, also known as junk bond funds; and if you want to keep down your tax bill, try municipal bond funds.

Valuing mutual funds

Most mutual funds are "open-end"—that means the fund will accept as much money as the public is willing to give it. The value of the fund—its net asset value (NAV)—is the total value of all the securities the fund owns divided by the number of fund shares.

If a mutual fund has a portfolio of stocks and bonds worth $10 million and the fund itself is divided into a million shares, the NAV would be $10. A mutual fund's NAV changes every day, depending on the price fluctuations of the holdings within the fund.

The NAV is the price at which you can buy and sell units of the fund—its shares, as long as you don't have to pay a sales commission, or "load." You may have to pay loads when you buy from a broker, financial planner, insurance agent or other adviser.

Avoid funds with high expenses

Any mutual fund can suffer poor performance for a quarter or even a year. But that won't hurt your long-term returns nearly as much as high expenses. So before you invest in a mutual fund, make sure its expenses are low. You need every possible bit of your return—you don't want to give too much of it to the mutual fund company.

Think about it. It costs money to run a mutual fund: there's research, administration, portfolio managers' salaries and so on. Those costs are passed along to you as a small percentage of total assets. The expenses may not seem like much—no more than a few percentage points a year—but they create a serious drag on performance over time.

Taxes, too, can take a big bite out of performance. If your mutual fund owns dividend-paying stocks, or if the fund manager sells some big winners, you'll owe your share of Uncle Sam's bill. Investors are often surprised to learn they owe taxes—both for dividends and for capital gains—even for funds that have declined in value. Tax-efficient mutual funds avoid activities that create short-term capital gains taxes, and minimize taxes by matching winning trades with losing ones.

Look for consistency in style and performance; don't chase returns

Remember, it's important to find the funds that match your goals. It's silly to chase today's top performers, because funds that rank highly over one period may not finish on top in later ones. After all, mutual funds may specialize in one area of investment, and no one area is always a winner.

When choosing among funds, look for consistent, long-term results and a stable investment style. If you've selected a small-cap stock fund, be sure the manager isn't dabbling in large-cap stocks just to boost the fund's return. It may seem good for the mutual fund, but that kind of "style drift" can distort your overall asset allocation.

Understand risk

We've talked a lot about volatility as a synonym for risk. And it's convenient shorthand for the most common investor concern—the uncertain value of investments in the short term. But there are other kinds of risk, too. They may be more or less important within a given asset class, but they do exist and you should be aware of them.

Let's take a look at some of the major kinds of investment risk.

Capital risk

Unless you are investing in a bond guaranteed by the U.S. government, you are putting your capital at risk each time you invest. No matter how small it is, there is some risk that you could lose your money.

Market risk

The risk that the value of your investment will decline in response to changes in investor sentiment, changes in the fortunes of the asset, changes in its industry or sector, or changes in the national economy overall. Market risk affects every market, from stocks and bonds to commodities and real estate.

Liquidity risk

The risk that you will not be able to sell an investment at the time you wish to do so. Tangible assets, such as real estate, carry an inherent liquidity risk. The risk is not only that you may be unable to sell the asset and put the proceeds of the sale into a more attractive investment, but also that you may be stuck holding an asset as it continues to decline in value.

Currency risk

This risk that movements in foreign currencies will change the value of your investment. Here's a simple example: Let's say you take a trip to Europe. To have some local cash in your pocket, you change $100 into euros. The euro is worth more than the dollar; it costs $1.25 to buy one euro, so your $100 buys you 80 euros (80 euros x $1.25 = $100). You have a great time sightseeing, but you don't spend any of the money—you put everything on credit cards. Just before you fly home, you change those euros in your pocket back into dollars. But in the week you've been overseas, the euro has fallen 20 percent. Now each euro is worth exactly $1.00. So you don't get back your $100; you only get back $80 (80 euros x $1.00 = $80). You've lost twenty bucks—you've just seen currency risk become reality.

The same risk applies to stocks and bonds purchased in foreign currencies. From rupee-denominated government bonds in India to rand-denominated South African mining stocks, any change in the value of those currencies relative to the dollar will affect the return on your investment, either for good or ill.

Currency risk also affects the stocks of U.S. companies that earn revenue from international sales. When the dollar is strong relative to other currencies, a company's overseas earnings are worth less when they are converted into dollars. Conversely, when the dollar is weak international sales become more meaningful, because each unit of the foreign currency is worth more dollars. In 2008, international sales accounted for more than half the revenue of the companies in the S&P 500.

Interest rate risk

As we explained earlier, fixed-income investments such as bonds lose value when interest rates rise. Why? Because the spread between the interest rate that the bond pays and the interest rate now charged to borrowers has narrowed, so the bond holder is no longer as far ahead as she was initially. Rising interest rates also increase the cost of doing business for most companies, make it more expensive for consumers to borrow and, as a result, tend to reduce demand—leading, often, to increased market risk.

Financial risk

This is the risk of financial troubles in the company in which you've invested. A few years ago, investors in Enron discovered just how serious it could be. A massive accounting fraud covered up the true shakiness of the company's financial situation. Investors, suddenly exposed to severe capital risk as well, lost their entire investment in the company.

Credit risk

This is the risk that a bond issuer will default and will not be able to repay interest and principal as promised. Credit risk is rarely a problem with government bonds, although municipalities—local governments—have defaulted on occasion. It is generally a risk associated with corporate bonds, as companies do go bankrupt.

Event risk

This is the risk of an unforeseen occurrence, from a political assassination to a tsunami, playing havoc with the markets. In a way, it's the risk that each of us accepts just getting out of bed in the morning.

By the way, if you elect not to participate in the market, then you're taking the biggest risk of all. You're assuring yourself of a declining standard of living, because inflation will eat away the value of your holdings over time. That's true even if you get a humongous raise or marry rich.

It's impossible to avoid risk—in investing or in life. But, as we've seen, risk can be managed. In fact, managing risk through asset allocation and diversification within and among asset classes is crucial to investment success.

Let's take a look at the common categories and sub-categories of stock mutual funds.

STOCK FUNDS

Value funds

Value fund managers look for stocks that they think are cheap relative to how much they earn or cheap relative to the value of the company's underlying assets.

Large-cap value managers typically look for big battered behemoths whose shares are selling at discounted prices. Often these managers have to hang on for a long time before their picks pan out. Top holdings might include such household names as Nike, Procter & Gamble, 3M, Kellogg and United Parcel Service.

Small-cap value managers typically bottom fish for small companies (usually ones with market value of less than $1 billion) that have been shunned or beaten down by other investors. They are often in sectors that are out of favor with the market (like construction in 2008) even though the companies themselves are poised to do well when conditions change.

Growth funds

Growth fund managers seek to invest in companies expected to grow more rapidly than their industry peers or more rapidly than stocks overall. There are many different breeds of growth funds. Some growth fund managers are content to buy shares in companies with mildly above-average revenue and earnings growth, while others, shooting for monster returns, try to catch the fastest growers before they crash.

Aggressive growth fund managers are like drag racers who keep the pedal to the metal while taking on some sizeable risk. These types of funds often lead the pack over long periods of time—as well as over short periods when the stock market is booming. They may make bets on small companies in areas such as medical technology, in which one breakthrough device can alter the landscape quickly and lead to a rapid rise in profits.

Growth fund managers also invest in shares of rapidly growing companies, but lean more toward large established names. Plus, growth managers are often willing to play it safe with cash. As a result, growth funds won't zoom as high in bull markets as their aggressive cousins, but they hold up a bit better when the market heads south. Typical investments might include Amazon, Apple, Genentech and other companies positioned to outperform their sectors and the economy at large.

Consider growth funds if you're seeking high long-term returns and can tolerate the normal ups and downs of the stock market. For most long-term investors, a growth fund should be the core holding around which the rest of their portfolio is built.

Growth-and-income, equity-income and balanced funds

These three types of funds have a common goal: providing steady long-term growth while simultaneously throwing off reliable income. They all hold some combination of dividend-paying stocks and income-producing securities, such as bonds or convertible securities (bonds or special types of stocks that pay interest but can also be converted into the company's regular shares).

None of the three types provide the growth potential of stock-only funds. While they tend to hold up better when the market turns sour, they lag in a raging bull market, when stocks can achieve high returns. In general, these funds are best for risk-averse investors and for those seeking current income without giving up the potential for some capital growth.

Growth-and-income funds concentrate more than the other two on growth, so they generally hold the lowest percentage of fixed-income investments.

Balanced funds strive to keep anywhere from 50 to 60 percent of their holdings in stocks and the rest in interest-paying securities such as bonds and convertibles, giving them the highest yields.

Equity-income funds are in the middle.

Sector and specialty funds

Rather than diversifying their holdings, sector and specialty funds concentrate their assets in a particular sector, such as technology or health care. There's nothing wrong with that approach, as long as you remember that one year's top sector could suffer a decline the following year. These funds are most appropriate for investors who are interested in a particular theme—say, biotech or alternative energy or aquaculture—but want to defray some of the risk of choosing individual stocks within the sector.

If you invest in sector funds, you may need to rotate them in and out of your portfolio more regularly than other kinds of funds. They're really a momentum play—taking advantage of the market's interest in a particular region or industry—and that momentum can fade or disappear as conditions change. With these funds in your portfolio, be prepared for plenty of care and feeding. They're definitely not a "set it and forget it" investment.

Now let's take a look at the universe of bond funds.

BOND FUNDS

A bond that you buy and hold is the perfect example of "set it and forget it." You get your coupon payment twice each year and your principal is returned at the bond's maturity. Bond funds, though, operate a little differently. They seek to juice the return by trading. By buying and selling between the issue date and the maturity date, they can improve the adjusted yield to maturity and give you a higher percentage gain on your investments.

This is not something you should try at home. Because even though bonds are conservative when bought at par and held to maturity, they can be pretty wild when they're actively traded. You can, if you're careful, trade *stocks* on your own—play the market, as they say. But no one "plays" the bond market. It's a world of fractions and levers in which each slight tick in interest rates—up or down—has a multiplier effect on the price, yield and sometimes even the issuer of the bond. If you're interested in potentially profiting from bond trading, do it through a professionally managed bond fund.

Let's look at some of the different kinds available to you.

U.S. government bond funds

These funds invest primarily in bonds issued by the U.S. Treasury or federal government agencies, which means you don't have to worry about credit risk. But because of their higher level of safety, their yields and total returns tend to be slightly lower than those of other bond funds.

That's not to say government bonds funds don't fluctuate—they do, right along with interest rates. If you can't tolerate swings of more than a few percentage points, stick to short-term government bond funds.

If fluctuations of 5 percent or so don't cause you to break out in a cold sweat, then you can pick up a bit more yield with intermediate government bond funds. If you plan on holding on for several years and can handle 10 percent swings, long-term government bond funds will provide even more yield.

Corporate bond funds

Funds in this category buy the bonds issued by corporations. These companies range from well-known household names to obscure widget makers most of us have never heard of. Note that the safest corporate bonds won't give you much more return than a government bond of similar duration.

When researching corporate bonds funds, consider the credit quality of the individual bonds they hold (most hold highly rated bonds, AAA to A minus or A3, but some take more risk by adding small doses of high-yielding junk bonds.) Also consider the average maturity of the bonds—the more time to maturity, the greater the volatility.

High-yield bond funds

Putting the euphemism aside, these are junk bond funds. They invest in debt of fledgling or small firms whose staying power is untested as well as in the bonds of large, respected companies in weakened financial condition. Bonds of the oldest, best-known companies can become junk if the market deems them risky.

The potential for these companies to default on their interest payments is much greater than on higher quality bonds, but since these funds usually hold more than 100 issues, a default here and there won't capsize the fund. In exchange for the risk, you get higher yields—usually 3 to 10 percentage points more than safer bond funds. These funds tend to shine when the economy is on a roll and suffer when the economy is fading, because the issuers, hurt by the down economy, face an increased risk of default.

High-yield or junk bond funds are most appropriate for investors seeking to boost their income and total returns and who are able to tolerate losses of 10 percent or so during periods of economic turbulence. Note that despite the "junk" appellation, the default rate on high-yield bonds is not so high compared with, say, the bankruptcy rate of publicly held Internet companies after the bubble burst. That could be small consolation, perhaps, but it does give some perspective.

Municipal bond funds

Tax-exempt bond funds—also known as muni bond funds—invest in the bonds issued by cities, states and other local government entities. As a result, they generate dividends that are free from federal income taxes.

The income from muni bond funds that invest only in the issues of a single state is also exempt from state and local taxes for resident shareholders. Once you factor in the tax benefits, muni funds often offer better yields than government and corporate bond funds, especially for investors in higher tax brackets.

INDEX FUNDS

The mutual funds we've been discussing are run by pros with specialized areas of knowledge. They buy and sell to get you the best returns. These "portfolio managers" have expertise you can't replicate. They have the time and experience to evaluate potential purchases and sales in ways you couldn't. Their abilities really shine in narrowly focused investment areas.

If you'd like to invest in retailers, for example, a professional manager will visit malls around the country and see which stores are doing well and which are doing poorly. She'll evaluate the company's management, its financial condition, whether it has labor or legal problems and more.

If you're interested in medical diagnostic equipment, you can invest in a fund that may be managed by a doctor who understands not only the equipment itself, but also the financing, insurance and administrative issues that will play a part in determining the future profitability of a company's new device. Perhaps the portfolio manager was formerly an administrator at a large hospital, or worked for an insurer, helping to draft their reimbursement policies for medical tests. These are real-life scenarios.

So you would think, then, that with the best business schools in the country churning out a steady supply of expensively educated MBAs who go to work for fund companies, mutual funds would have no trouble posting above-average returns. After all, fund shareholders (that's you) are paying fund managers big bucks to find the best stocks in the market.

The surprising fact is, however, most mutual funds don't beat the market. You'd be better off buying all the stocks in the Standard & Poor's 500 index or in the Wilshire 5000 index (which includes just about every stock on the New York, American and Nasdaq stock exchanges) than paying someone to select what he or she thinks are the best ones.

That's the idea behind an index fund. Index funds track the performance of market benchmarks, such as the S&P 500, the Dow, Nasdaq, etc. Such "passive" funds offer a number of advantages over "active" funds: unlike actively managed funds, there's no high-priced manager deciding what to buy. Because of that, index funds tend to charge lower expenses and be more tax efficient, and there's no risk the fund manager will make sudden changes that throw off your portfolio's allocation.

The individual probably most responsible for the development of index funds is John C. Bogle, the founder of the Vanguard Group.

The birth of index funds

Some time back, it occurred to Bogle that investors were being hurt three ways by traditional "actively managed" mutual funds. First, investors' desire to always achieve the best returns ultimately wounded them. They'd chase a successful manager and then, when his or her star had faded, seek another. Buying and selling funds cost money, and very few managers could provide superior returns for extended periods.

Second, the fund's expenses—the costs involved in having these managers actively buy and sell securities—often took 2 percent or more off the top of a fund's return. If a fund returned 10 percent, investors made eight. Third, the churning of the fund—the constant buying and selling of securities as it frantically sought high returns—generated trading costs that were passed along to investors and, in addition, generated capital gains on which taxes had to be paid.

Bogle had an idea: instead of trying to beat the market, why not replicate it? Since the S&P 500—a market-weighted basket of the stocks of 500 leading U.S. companies—returned an average of 10 percent per year, why not create a fund that mimicked it? All you'd have to do, he reasoned, was purchase the same stocks in the same proportion as the S&P 500.

True, the S&P 500 wasn't actually a fund. It was a concept, a hypothetical basket of securities that served as a proxy for the overall economic performance of the country. You couldn't really own it. "Well," said Bogle as he set about assembling the basket for real, "you can own it now." And once he put it together, he didn't touch it. Barely looked at it. Didn't try to goose performance of any single element; he just left it alone.

The logic of index funds

Bogle's index fund was a resounding success. There was something so appealingly logical about it. There wasn't the constant buying and selling that characterized actively managed funds. The fund wasn't always spinning off tax-generating capital gains, and it wasn't filled with up-front charges and back-end charges and fees that ripped the sweetest part of an investor's returns right off the top. Instead, because it didn't cost a lot of money to manage the fund—basically, the manager just had to come in to the office each morning and make sure his screen was still plugged in—the ratio of expenses to assets was only 0.18 percent (eighteen one-hundredths of 1 percent!). Investors kept much more of their return than they did with actively managed funds, and over time, thanks to the power of compounding, that money added up.

Soon other index funds were created. Some tracked the

Dow. Some replicated the Russell 2000, which tracks small-cap companies. Other funds were created to bring index investing to bond funds. Today, there are hundreds of index funds that track sectors, industries, countries, regions and entire markets around the world.

There's another reason passive investing (index investing) makes sense in so many situations. The majority of the return earned by stock and bond funds is not dependent on the skill of the individual manager; it's driven more by the direction of the market overall. Yes, there are disciplines in which manager skill is key to success—hedge fund investments, for example. But in the stock and bond markets, a rising tide lifts all boats and a hurricane batters both the good and the bad.

There are some caveats. Indexing seems to work best in large transparent markets, like those for U.S. stocks and bonds. Because there is so much information on these big securities, it's tough for a fund manager to gain an edge on the market. But in emerging markets, or in newer industries such as alternative energy or genetically enhanced foods, the story may be different. In those instances, certain managers may have access to information that others don't, and they can act on this information to produce superior returns.

A quick word about short selling

"Long only" is the way we have traditionally talked about investments—we expect them to appreciate. We buy on the expectation of rising prices and we sell on the expectation of decline. We may tolerate negative performance in stocks and bonds, but we certainly don't welcome it. We make our money when the market does well.

But there's another kind of investing, short selling, which represents the inverse of this vision. Short sellers do well when the market falls. It's a little bit complicated, but stay with me, because it's interesting.

Let's say there's a company called Orcas and they make cute little molded plastic shoes, kind of like flip-flops only different. For some inexplicable reason, celebrities have latched onto the shoe: in fact, in the supermarket magazines just last week you saw photos of movie stars wearing them and now they're everywhere. Curious, you check out the company online and you see that shares of its stock have gone from $20 to $80 in five months. A four-fold increase! Unreal!

The first thing you think is that you wish you'd bought the stock at $20. But wait a minute here. How's this little company going to meet this huge demand? Isn't it likely to have problems with its supply chain? Won't it have to borrow money to expand its operations? Isn't that money going to be more expensive in today's higher interest rate environment? If demand is that strong, won't other companies try to horn in with their own, cheaper versions of the shoe? And don't celebrities—and the public—get tired of fads? You do the math and realize that the current stock price can only be justified if every man, woman and child on the planet buys three pairs of Orcas. In just a few minutes, you decide that Orcas is overvalued and due for a fall. You take steps to "short" the stock.

Here's what you do. You borrow 1,000 shares of Orcas promising to repay it at a future date. Your broker arranges the transaction, and you pay him a small fee for the service. You immediately take the shares and sell them at $80 apiece. Now you go on with your life, checking the stock price of Orcas each day. Remember, you're still on the hook to return 1,000 shares that you don't own. At some point, you'll have to give them back.

But what's this? One day, you wake up, turn on CNN and learn that Orcas stock has fallen 50 percent. The company has had production problems. When Orcas misses its delivery dates, stores cancel their orders, driving the price down further. Two weeks later, the stock drops to $30 a share. This is your moment. You buy 1,000 shares and give them to the individual or company that loaned them to you in the first place. You've just made $50,000—the difference between selling the 1,000 shares you borrowed at $80 a share and replacing them with 1,000 shares you bought for $30 a share. That's short selling.

It's dangerous, though. What if you were wrong? What if, instead of going from $80 to $30, shares had gone from $80 to $160? Think of how sick you'd feel as you watched the price climb each day. You can see that short selling is not for the faint of heart.

Since there's no ceiling on how high the shares can go, your potential risk would be unlimited. On the other hand, there is a ceiling on how much you can make—it's the difference between the price at which you borrow the stock and zero.

But the most important difference between long invest-ing and short selling may be this: in long-only investing—the kind we've been discussing—your loss is limited to your total investment. In other words, you can't lose more than all your money. (I know that sounds weird, positioning a statement like that as a positive.) In short selling, though, you can lose much more money than you invested. You can find that you owe money in quantities you never dreamed of. In our Orcas example, you have to replace those shares no matter how high they go—even if they cost $1,000 each. Or more. That's why it's probably best to leave short selling to the pros.

If you're really intrigued by short selling, there are mutual funds whose managers specialize in that discipline. It's a safer way to participate, because you get the potential benefits of short selling, but your risk is limited to the amount of your investment.

BLENDED AND ALTERNATIVE FUNDS

These mutual funds seek positive returns in all market environments. In other words, whether the market goes up or down, they want to make money. (Don't we all.)

Now, a stock or a bond generally does well when the overall stock or bond market is doing well. An individual stock or bond may over- or under-perform its broader market, but it's unusual for a stock to be up 10 percent, say, if the overall market is down 15 percent. In fact, the main determinants of stock returns are, in order: overall stock market performance, sector performance, company performance.

So if you own McDonald's, your performance will be influenced by the market, the fast-food business overall and then how McDonald's is doing relative to its direct competitors and in the context of its own internal issues.

OK. There are investments out there that try to counter the effects of overall market direction, so that you can benefit even in a down market. While these investments try to capture some upside, they exist mainly to protect you from market declines.

Imagine that you're a pension fund. A pension fund pays pensions—retirement benefits—to hundreds of thousands of people on an ongoing basis. Come hell or high water, you've got to be able to cover your payments every month, year in and year out.

So if you're that pension fund, you don't care about investing your assets so that they earn the highest return in a good year. All you care about is making sure you've got enough money in your account when it's time to send out the checks.

Why not just invest in bonds, you ask? Because in a low interest rate environment, you may not be able to buy bonds that will offer sufficient return to cover the checks you have to write. To meet your payments, you need more upside, but you can't afford an equal amount of downside risk. That's where balanced and alternative investments come in.

The simplest form of balanced investment is a mutual fund that holds both stocks and bonds. The fund manager can alter the balance depending on her view of the market. The stocks provide growth opportunity and the bonds offset some of the risk. In difficult market conditions, the fund may lose some money, but not nearly as much as an all-stock fund. In good times, the fund won't rise as high as an all-stock fund, either. It's the old risk and return story.

An alternative fund, such as a market-neutral, long-short

equity, or bear fund, is a more refined version of the balanced concept. But instead of offsetting stock risk by buying bonds, a manager will attempt to reduce risk by buying some stocks "long" and "shorting" others. As we explained, "shorting," or short selling, is an attempt to profit from the anticipated decline in the value of a stock or bond. It's a common tool of hedge fund traders.

In fact, the original idea of hedge funds was to create an investment that could offer predictable returns in all market conditions. It's only recently, thanks to leverage—the ability to borrow money to increase the size of the bet—that hedge funds have produced such outsize returns and seen such spectacular and bloody crashes.

But in a market-neutral fund, or a long-short fund (a type of market-neutral fund), the manager is simply trying to hedge, or protect, against a bad market.

Perhaps the manager sees an opportunity in Coke versus Pepsi. Perhaps she reads that several large international bottlers have decided to stop working with Pepsi and sign a more lucrative agreement with Coke. She believes this helps Coke and hurts Pepsi in the fast-growing Asia-Pacific region, where the public can't seem to quench its thirst for soft drinks. So the manager buys shares of Coke long and shorts a similar value of Pepsi shares. The manager is hoping to profit on the future difference between shares of Coke and shares of Pepsi regardless of what happens in the overall market.

In this example, Coke and Pepsi don't have to move in opposite directions for the manager to profit. The manager's bet pays off as long as Coke does better than Pepsi, up or down.

That's the idea of market-neutral funds, long-short funds, bear funds and all the others that try to eliminate the effects of market direction—often called *beta*—from their returns. They seek to benefit from the skill of the manager alone. This part of the return—called *alpha*—is the manager's holy grail. In our Coke-Pepsi example, the manager is playing one company against the other. Even if the market falls, the manager profits if she has correctly calibrated the difference between the future share prices of the two firms. She's removed market risk and zeroed in on a deal where her judgment alone will determine the outcome.

There are many variations of this game. Long-short funds bet on companies. Global macro funds expand the field, seeking opportunities wherever they may occur—in foreign currencies, industrial metals, sovereign debt, you name it. And it doesn't have to be Coke versus Pepsi. It could just as easily be Tiffany jewelry versus John Deere tractors, or an entire industry versus another. The key is a bet on the divergence in future price between a pair of stocks, bonds, commodities or what have you. It's an attempt to offset risk in one area with a counterbalancing, opposite-weighted trade in another.

If you have a 401(k) plan at work, chances are you don't have any alternative funds on your menu of choices. You can still invest in them outside your retirement savings structure. But because these funds do so much buying and selling, they create taxable gains frequently. So the benefit of the funds may be somewhat diminished by the taxes you might have to pay.

If you have an IRA however, there are few restrictions on the investments you can hold, and I would urge you to consider alternative funds for a portion of your retirement portfolio. Again, the money will grow tax-free for as long as it's in the IRA. When you withdraw, you'll pay income tax on the withdrawal. You won't pay tax on past activity in the account itself.

EXCHANGE TRADED FUNDS (ETFs)

Exchange traded funds (we'll call them ETFs) are index mutual funds that trade just like stocks. Want to invest in the market quickly and cheaply? ETFs are the most practical vehicle. All the major stock indexes have ETFs based on them, including the Dow Jones Industrial Average, the Standard & Poor's 500 Index and the Nasdaq Composite.

ETFs have been called the most innovative investment product of the past 20 years. They offer many of the benefits of standard index funds—low costs relative to other investments, tax efficiency, diversification, transparency—but they have other advantages as well.

For starters, they can expose you to opportunities that were formerly too difficult to access. Large-cap stocks in Japan? Sure. Timber and mining companies in Indonesia? No problem. Technology in Scandinavia? You betcha. Today, you can get ETFs that track broad-based indexes, international and country-specific indexes, industry- and sector-specific indexes, bond indexes and commodity indexes. There are ETFs for large U.S. companies, small ones, Real Estate Investment Trusts (REITs), international stocks, bonds and even gold. Pick an asset class that is publicly available and there is a good bet that it is represented by an ETF or will be soon.

ETFs have some fundamental differences from traditional mutual funds. Traditional mutual funds take orders during Wall Street trading hours, but the transactions actually occur at the close of the market. The price they receive is the sum of the closing day prices of all the stocks contained in the fund. ETFs, by contrast, trade instantaneously all day long and allow an investor to lock in a price for the underlying stocks immediately.

ETFs are economical to buy and maintain over the long run, making them especially attractive for the typical investor. Annual fees are as low as .09 percent of assets, which is breathtakingly low compared to the average mutual fund fees of 1.4 percent. You could build an entire, well-diversified portfolio using nothing but ETFs.

Because ETFs are sold through brokers, you have to pay a transaction fee to purchase them, but they're still not expensive relative to other investments. And, while it's beyond the scope of this book, it's worth noting that they're very useful to hedge fund managers, because options based on ETFs allow for various defensive—or speculative—investing strategies.

Do your homework!

I hope it goes without saying that you owe it to yourself to do some research before you put your money in any investment. In-depth mutual fund information is widely available, either from the funds themselves, from third-party ratings companies like Morningstar, or by using CNNMoney.com's mutual-fund screening tool. Just to review, here are some things to look out for:

1. *Opt for funds with low expenses.* Fund expenses directly reduce your returns, so you'll increase your odds of success by avoiding funds with bloated expense ratios.

In addition to their management expenses, many mutual funds have transaction fees, sales loads and marketing and advertising expenses, all of which are paid by the investor. Just to set the record straight, transaction fees are charged by the mutual fund company when you buy or sell shares; up-front or back-end sales loads are, in essence, commissions paid to the broker who sells the funds on behalf of the fund company; and marketing and advertising are folded into 12b-1 fees. These fees and expenses come off the top and can make an investor's actual return lower than the stated return earned by the manager.

It's worth looking at expenses relative to the return you expect, because their impact can vary. A large-cap stock fund returns about 10 percent, so a 1 percent expense ratio effectively eats 10 percent of your return. With a bond fund, which returns 8 percent on average, that one percent expense ratio takes 12.5 percent of your earnings. And in a money market fund, with an expected return of 5 percent, that 1 percent expense ratio equals 20 percent of your return. So you can see that while 1 percent may not sound like much in the abstract, expenses have a very negative, very concrete effect on your investment returns.

2. *Look for consistency of style.* For a fund to fit into a diversified portfolio, it's important that the manager stick to a particular investing style. If you bought a fund because you

want your portfolio to include, say, small value stocks, then you don't want a fund manager jumping into large stock issues.

3. *Consider risk.* Returns may vary, but funds that are risky tend to stay risky. So be sure to check out the route the fund took to rack up past gains and decide whether you would be comfortable with such a ride. Here are some risk measures to consider:

Beta measures how much a fund's value jumps around in relation to changes in the value of the S&P 500 index, which by definition has a beta of 1.0. A stock fund with a beta of 1.20 is 20 percent more volatile than the S&P 500—that is, for every move in the S&P 500, the fund will move 20 percent more in either direction, up or down.

Standard deviation tells you how much a fund fluctuates from its own average returns. A standard deviation of 10 means the fund's monthly returns usually fall within 10 percentage points of its average. The higher the standard deviation, the more volatile the fund.

Worst quarter is a very straightforward measure of risk: it merely shows the fund's worst quarterly return on record, giving you a feel of what to brace yourself for.

4. *Check out past performance relative to peers.* If you're investing in an actively managed fund rather than an index fund or ETF, you should look at its long-term record (at least three years and preferably five years) versus that of its peers, as well as how it has fared over shorter stretches. Compare those results

to category averages—you can't really fault a small-cap fund manager for a lousy year if all small-cap funds did poorly. But it's a lot harder to be forgiving if a fund does much worse than all its peers, especially if it does so over a sustained period.

5. *Seek low taxes.* You can't forget about taxes just because you don't have any intention of selling your fund shares. As a fund owner, you also own all the stocks in the fund's portfolio. If the fund manager sells a stock for a huge capital gain, you'll have to report that gain on your tax return. This doesn't apply to gains in a tax-sheltered retirement account, of course.

6. *When investing in stock funds, steer clear of asset bloat.* This is more of an issue with small-cap funds than with large-cap funds. The latter buy big stocks with a lot of shares, so the manager shouldn't have too much of a problem buying more GE and IBM when investors pour money into the fund.

But since small-cap funds are buying stocks with very few shares, an extra billion or two from new mutual fund buyers like you can tie the manager's hands. To put the additional money to work, the small-cap fund manager may have to drop his standards or accumulate overly large positions in individual stocks.

7. *When investing in bond funds, stick with short to intermediate bond maturities.* Over the past 20 years or so, long-term bond funds have provided the highest returns, partly because interest rates have steadily declined over that period. But that may not always be the case. What's more, long-term bond

funds can be surprisingly volatile. If interest rates rise just 1 percentage point, a long-term bond fund can drop 10 percent or more, wiping out more than a year's interest.

So if you're investing for 10 years or less, or if you're using bond funds to add some ballast to a predominantly stock portfolio, you may be better off with bond funds with short- to intermediate-term maturities—say, 5 to 10 years. You can typically get 75 to 80 percent of the return of long-term funds, while incurring roughly 40 percent less volatility. And remember, lower volatility per unit of return is your goal.

8. *Beware of tempting bond yields.* Fund companies know that investors focus on yields. So some do everything they can short of putting the fund on steroids to pump up yields. They may throw some low-grade bonds into a government portfolio, or even invest in international bonds from countries where rates are especially high.

These ploys to boost interest may or may not pay off, but they all involve risks that are difficult to evaluate. A bond fund that's touting much higher yields than funds with similar maturities raises red flags—it's a sign that the fund is doing something much different, and probably much riskier, than its peers. If a much higher-yielding offering can't explain its out-sized yields by having ultra-low expenses, move on (or accept the fact that you're investing in a riskier-than-average fund).

Selling when the time is right

You shouldn't sell a mutual fund just because it has a bad year.

If the overall market is down, or the specific sector your fund invests in is out of favor, you can't expect your fund manager to be a miracle worker. But there are circumstances that should make you consider other investments. Among them are the following:

1. *Your fund is a persistent loser.* If you own a fund that trails similar funds for two years by a substantial margin—say, 2 percentage points or more—think about moving on.

2. *The fund's investment strategy has changed.* If you've attempted to create a diversified portfolio, then you're probably counting on the managers of all your funds to invest a certain way. The small-cap fund manager should be sticking to small-cap stocks, and the large-cap value fund manager should be buying large-cap value stocks. If they stray, it puts your entire plan in jeopardy.

3. *There's been a manager change.* Any time your fund gets a new skipper, you should closely monitor the situation to assure two things: first, that the new manager is following the same investing style and strategy as his predecessor; second, that performance hasn't suffered. Give a new manager one year (and no more than two) to prove herself.

4. *You could use the tax loss.* There are times when you might be able to lower your tax bill by dumping a losing fund yet still pretty much maintain your asset mix. For example, say you own shares in a large-cap growth fund that are worth

less than you paid for them. If you sell, you can use the loss to offset gains in other securities. Then, you can turn right around and buy another large-cap growth fund. Or, you can buy back the very same fund after 31 days (by law, you have to stay out of a fund you've sold for 31 days before buying back into it).

$$$ WHAT DID WE LEARN? $$$

1.   Mutual funds, index funds and ETFs provide the greatest diversification for each dollar invested.

When you buy into a fund, you essentially buy all the underlying stocks or bonds that the fund holds. You diversify among multiple companies and/or multiple bond issuers, lowering your risk and increasing your opportunity to achieve superior returns.

2.   Seek funds with low expenses.

Expenses can significantly lower investment performance. Mutual funds with high expense ratios can take more than 2 percent of your return. If your fund has a return of 9 percent, for example, and expenses take 2 percent, you're giving up 22 percent (two-ninths) of your return. That's a big chunk, and over time, it will make a significant difference in your investment earnings.

3.   Index funds and ETFs generally have the lowest expenses.

Because index funds and ETFs are passively managed, they do not have significant trading costs or manager salaries. They seek to replicate, not exceed, the returns of the markets they track, and they achieve their objectives at a low cost to investors.

4. Evaluate a fund carefully before you decide to sell it.

Any fund can have a bad year. But if a fund lags its peers consistently, changes its style, replaces its manager or spends too much time near the bottom of its category over a two-year period, you may want to replace it.

5. Market-neutral funds seek positive performance in good times and bad.

Market-neutral funds, long-short funds, bear funds and balanced funds attempt to provide "all weather" returns by focusing on the skill of the manager rather than the performance of the overall market. By combining "long" and "short" bets, the manager seeks to offset risk and deliver high upside potential with low downside risk.

Coming up...

Funds, whether actively or passively managed, are the right investment choice for most individual investors. They can provide diversification within asset classes, bring you access to opportunities around the globe and offer expertise in unfamiliar markets. If you have neither the time nor the tools to do your own detailed research, mutual funds, index funds and ETFs should be the components of your portfolio.

Now that we've identified the building blocks, let's construct your future.

7 | BUILDING YOUR CUSTOM-TAILORED PORTFOLIO

"Nature gave man two ends—one to sit on, and one to think with. Even since then man's success or failure has been dependent on the one he used most."

– George R. Kirkpatrick (1867-1937)

Now it's time to meet the star of this book—you. Everything you've read so far is just a prelude to the main story: building the investment portfolio that's going to take you where you want to go. What will it look like? What will be in it? It's completely your call. And to help you make it, I'm going to walk you through the steps you need to consider before you start to buy assets.

We've seen that there are smart ways to invest in any asset class. And we know that combining asset classes is the best way to ensure a steady return on your investments. Further, we've learned that even volatile assets do well over time (in fact, they perform best over time).

So the strategy you follow should be a function of your investment time horizon—how many years you'll be contributing to your portfolio before you start taking money out of it—and your ability to tolerate volatility. After all, you've got to be comfortable with the decisions you make. If you had money in the market in stocks in the fall of 2008 and you were able to sleep soundly every night, you probably have a good tolerance for volatility. If you woke up and paced the floor at 3:00 A.M. each morning, you might not.

To help you decide what's best for your situation, Doug Flynn, Certified Financial Planner™, Chartered Financial Consultant, and partner and co-founder of Flynn Zito Capital Management, LLC, has worked with me to construct five model portfolios. Each portfolio corresponds to a certain set of life criteria, but the two most important determinants of the portfolio appropriate for you are age and attitude toward volatility.

There are mild-mannered individuals who wouldn't dream of playing chess without a helmet but who can handle short-term market gyrations without flinching. And there are seasoned bungee jumpers 25 years from retirement who can't accept even the possibility of losses in two consecutive quarters. So you can see that there's a psychological component to investing that overlays the rational parts of the equation.

We'll define the five investor segments by risk tolerance and portfolio objectives, like this:

Very High Risk Tolerance (Aggressive Growth)

Most suitable for those with the longest time horizon (under age 34) who focus on the highest long-term growth without regard for investment income and who can tolerate potential loss of principal in exchange for the potentially highest returns.

High Risk Tolerance (Growth)

Most suitable for those with a long time horizon (ages 35–44) who focus on strong growth without regard for investment income and who can accept some declines in value in exchange for potentially higher returns.

Moderate Risk Tolerance (Growth with Income)

Most suitable for those with a medium-term time horizon (ages 45–54) who seek moderate growth and stable income, and who can tolerate small drops in value during difficult market conditions.

Low Risk Tolerance (Income with Moderate Growth)

Most suitable for those with a shorter time until retirement (ages 55–64) who seek cautious growth and steady income and who find it difficult to tolerate portfolio declines.

Very Low Risk Tolerance (Income)

Most suitable for investors near or in retirement (ages 65+) who are focused on stability, small profits and the protection of principal.

Let's start with a simple self-test to assess which portfolio will be most appropriate for your situation. We'll call it the Velshi Volatility Test, because it will—I hope—help you make decisions from a more informed perspective.

Your investment questionnaire

The test has seven questions, and each answer is awarded one to five points. The five point answer is always at the top of each question; the one point answer at the bottom. At the end of the test, add up your numbers and I'll tell you what they mean. Ready? Here we go.

Time horizon

1. How old are you?

a. Under age 34 (5 points)

b. 35–44 (4 points)

c. 45–54 (3 points)

d. 55–64 (2 points)

e. 65 or older (1 point)

2. When do you expect to start withdrawing from your portfolio?

a. Not for at least 20 years (5 points)

b. In 10 to 20 years (4 points)

c. In 5 to 10 years (3 points)

d. Within 5 years (2 points)

e. Immediately (1 point)

Goals and expectations

3. Which statement best describes your long-term investment objectives?

a. I'm willing to accept substantial risk and potential loss of principal in exchange for the highest potential long-term gains. (5 points)

b. I want to build my nest egg and will accept some losses on the way to potentially higher returns. (4 points)

c. I'm looking for a balance between growth and stability without too much fluctuation around my targeted return. (3 points)

d. I want to grow with caution. I can tolerate small, short-term losses but I'm concerned about protecting my money. (2 points)

e. I want to avoid losing money. My main concerns are safety and a stable return. (1 point)

4. Assuming normal market conditions, what would you expect from this investment over time?

a. To generally keep pace with the stock market (5 points)

b. To slightly trail the stock market, but make a good profit (4 points)

c. To trail the stock market but make a moderate profit (3 points)

d. To have some stability but make modest profits (2 points)

e. To have a high degree of stability but make small profits (1 point)

5. Suppose the stock market performs unusually poorly over the next decade. What would you expect to happen to your portfolio?

a. It would lose money (5 points)

b. It would make very little or nothing (4 points)

c. It would eke out a little gain (3 points)

d. It would come out slightly ahead (2 points)

e. It would be little affected by what happens in the stock market (1 point)

Short-term risk attitudes

6. Which of these statements would best describe your attitude about the next three years' performance of the investment?

a. I'm in it for the long term. Whatever happens, happens (5 points)

b. I can tolerate a loss because I've got time to make it up (4 points)

c. I can tolerate a small loss (3 points)

d. I'd have a hard time tolerating any losses (2 points)

e. I need to see at least a little return (1 point)

7. Which of these statements would best describe your attitude about the next three months' performance of this investment?

a. Who cares? Three months means nothing (5 points)

b. I wouldn't worry too much about losses in that time frame (4 points)

c. If I suffered a loss of greater than 10 percent, I'd be concerned (3 points)

d. I'd be worried about any loss of more than a few points (2 points)

e. I'd have a hard time accepting any losses (1 point)

You're done! Enter total score: _____

What you've done is answered questions about three issues that affect investment decisions: time horizon, long-term goals and short-term risk attitudes. Here's how your total score matches up with our model portfolios:

32-35:   *Very High Risk (Aggressive Growth) Portfolio*

25-31:   *High Risk (Moderately Aggressive Growth) Portfolio*

18-24:   *Moderate Risk (Growth with Income) Portfolio*

11-17:   *Low Risk (Income with Moderate Growth) Portfolio*

7-10:   *Very Low Risk (Income with Capital Preservation) Portfolio*

Remember, there are no right or wrong answers to any of these questions. Except for your age, the questions are completely subjective—they're about your attitudes and expectations. A further caveat is that each of us interprets words differently. One person's idea of "moderate growth" or "small losses" may be unlike another's. So this test is only a guide to get you thinking about the implications of the decisions you will make. No matter how you answered, you did great.

Your model portfolios

Now let's take a look at the portfolios that suit your risk tolerance.

While an IRA allows you to buy pretty much any regulated investment out there, your 401(k) or 403(b) investment choices will be far more limited. The names of those funds may not correspond to the categories listed here. But a quick check on Morningstar, or a call to the company that administers your plan, will tell you which funds fit into the categories you need.

VERY HIGH RISK
AGGRESSIVE GROWTH

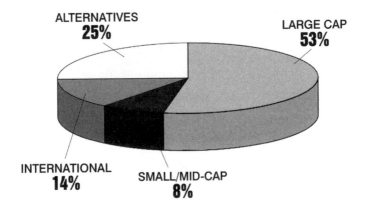

ALTERNATIVES
25%

LARGE CAP
53%

INTERNATIONAL
14%

SMALL/MID-CAP
8%

Based on historical averages this portfolio
has an expected annual rate of return of
11.50%

Source: Flynn Zito Capital Management, LLC

HIGH RISK
MODERATELY AGGRESSIVE GROWTH

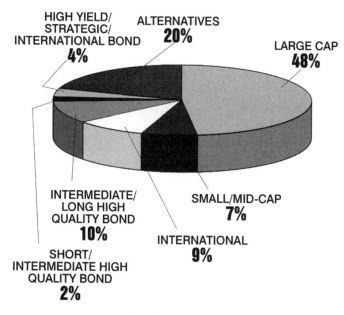

Based on historical averages this portfolio
has an expected annual rate of return of
9.75%

Source: Flynn Zito Capital Management, LLC

MODERATE RISK
GROWTH WITH INCOME

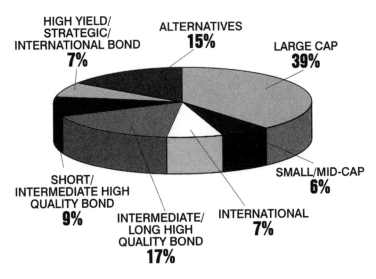

Based on historical averages this portfolio
has an expected annual rate of return of
8.25%

LOW RISK
INCOME WITH MODERATE GROWTH

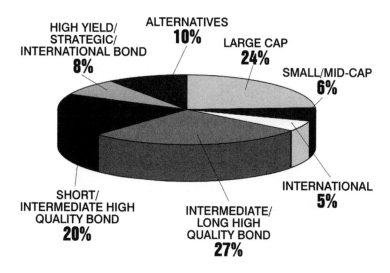

HIGH YIELD/ STRATEGIC/ INTERNATIONAL BOND 8%

ALTERNATIVES 10%

LARGE CAP 24%

SMALL/MID-CAP 6%

INTERNATIONAL 5%

SHORT/ INTERMEDIATE HIGH QUALITY BOND 20%

INTERMEDIATE/ LONG HIGH QUALITY BOND 27%

Based on historical averages this portfolio
has an expected annual rate of return of
7.00%

Source: Flynn Zito Capital Management, LLC

VERY LOW RISK
INCOME WITH CAPITAL PRESERVATION

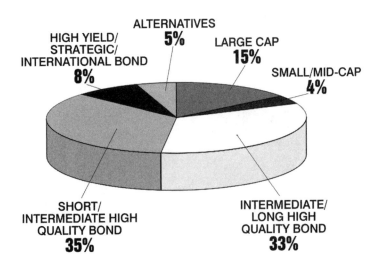

ALTERNATIVES **5%**

HIGH YIELD/
STRATEGIC/
INTERNATIONAL BOND
8%

LARGE CAP **15%**

SMALL/MID-CAP **4%**

SHORT/
INTERMEDIATE HIGH
QUALITY BOND
35%

INTERMEDIATE/
LONG HIGH
QUALITY BOND
33%

Based on historical averages this portfolio
has an expected annual rate of return of
5.59%

Source: Flynn Zito Capital Management, LLC

You can see that the portfolios contain all the asset classes we've discussed, except for cash. That's because we've assumed your cash is sitting on the side, in a separate account where you can take what you need when you need it. (For beating inflation, cash doesn't work for you all that well.)

In stocks, we've diversified by both company size and by regions; within bonds, we've diversified by duration and bond quality.

You'll notice, also, that the three middle portfolios use exactly the same asset classes, but their proportions vary in order to meet the differing portfolio objectives. It's a good example of the way we're putting asset allocation to work.

In fact, we could show these allocations even more precisely. We could break down our large- and small-cap stocks into growth and value segments, and we could divide our international stocks into large and small-cap components. But for the purposes of this illustration, I thought we'd keep it on the easy-to-grasp side, more of a "this is how it's done" than an explicit "do this."

We've also used alternatives in all five portfolios. As you remember, they're great diversifiers because they're not highly correlated to stocks or bonds. And they can provide stock-like returns with bond-like volatility.

If you're setting up your portfolio as a taxable account, not a retirement account, you might want to fill the bond allocations with tax-free bonds where possible. Especially if you're in a high tax bracket. You might also consider using tax-advantaged mutual funds in the stock portion of the portfolio.

You can use these models as a general guide in creating

your own portfolio. Simply fill in the slices of the pie with the investment vehicles you choose and you're on your way. They can be active funds, index funds or ETFs. You can build a portfolio from your company's 401(k) offerings.

If you're building your portfolio with mutual funds, though, remember that you might not be able to use the fund's name to determine in which "slice" it belongs. You can check Morningstar or the mutual fund screener at CNNmoney.com to see the fund's actual category.

You can—and sometimes should—have more than one fund in each category, but you should do it to diversify, not duplicate, your other holdings. For example, if you have an S&P 500 index fund, you probably don't also need a large cap stock fund. But owning both a transportation stock index fund and a retail stock index fund makes more sense, because they'll have different holdings.

The importance of rebalancing

Remember that both you and your portfolio will change as time goes by. You'll get older and your time until retirement will grow shorter. And not every slice of your portfolio pie will grow at the same rate. So it's a good idea to examine your portfolio each year and re-balance your assets in light of those changes. There are two reasons for this:

1. Your portfolio assets will grow at different rates

2. Your risk tolerance will change over time

If, for example, you allocated 8 percent to small and midcap stocks and they grew so fast they're now 11 percent, you'll want to take some of that money and move it so that the actual portfolio composition is in line with your objectives. It's hard to sell winners; your natural instinct is to buy more of them. But to maintain the proper portfolio balance, there will be times when you'll have to sell assets that go up and buy the ones that didn't.

If you don't think you've got the strength for counter-intuitive buying and selling, you might want to consider lifestyle and target date funds. These are mutual funds that are, in effect, model portfolios calibrated to your age. All you have to do is pick a projected retirement year and the fund managers do the rest. They adjust their asset mix as you get older, tracking you through life, dialing down the risk level as you get closer to retirement. Target-date funds can be excellent choices for people who prefer to leave decisions to the experts. The fund managers can make the tough buy and sell decisions without emotion.

It's not just your age that can change your risk profile. You'll want to adjust your portfolio mix to reflect your evolving goals. Marriage, a child, a home—life isn't static. Investing isn't static, either. So ride herd on those investments—don't let them stray off the trail.

I'd suggest you review your portfolio every quarter. Pick a comfortable time, a comfortable chair and look over your account. The key is to leave emotion out of it—whether they're up or down, quarterly returns are too short-term to get excited about. But it's important to stay involved with your finances.

After all, it's your future we're talking about. Don't make rash decisions, but don't be afraid to change. And please, don't do something just because your brother-in-law did. Your portfolio is for you. It reflects your individual situation.

While I recommend reviewing your portfolio each quarter, you may not need to rebalance it more than once a year. Needs change. You'll want to make sure your portfolio addresses the person you are, not the person you were. Each year, some fine-tuning is likely to be necessary, even if it's only to bring your current holdings into line with the allocation you established 12 months ago. In many years it will amount to little more than gardening, pruning the assets that have grown quickly and watering those that, for one reason or another, lag expectations. But in certain years you will have had major life changes, and in those cases, you'll want to revisit—and maybe revise—your asset allocation overall.

Financial advisers: yes or no?

A word here about financial advisers. The question is, "Are they worth it?" The answer, not surprisingly, is, "It depends."

That's not a cop-out. It has more to do with you than the advisor. What's interesting is that there are many areas of life where we wouldn't dream of not using a trained professional. Anyone here want to take out your own appendix? Raise your hands. I thought not.

Many of us are quite willing to hire carpenters to modernize our kitchens, golf pros to help improve our games, tutors to give our kids a better shot at Harvard and, of course, barbers and hairdressers to help us look our best.

But when it comes to the most important decisions about arguably the most important area of our lives—our futures—the attitude is often, "Why the hell should I pay some joker to do something I can do myself?"

Now, granted, there are true do-it-yourselfers in this world. They've got the *TIME Life* series of home improvement books and they can fix the bathroom sink, stop the squeak in the front door, seal the drafty window and all the rest. They not only knit their own sweaters, they shear the sheep and card the wool. They've put the household finances on Quicken and they enjoy sitting at the computer, paying the bills electronically and roaming through the fields of their orderly, buttoned-up realm.

But then there are the rest of us. We tend to go with the flow. We don't read all the instructions before we try to assemble the toy. If no one's stolen our identity, it's probably because no one's interested, not because we've been especially careful about it. When we look at what's involved in perfection, we usually decide that close enough is good enough.

Certainly the latter group, and probably the former as well, could benefit from the services of a professional who knows the terrain and whose job it is to help you stay out of the swamp and walk a safe and comfortable path to long-term financial security.

Financial planners can help you access opportunities you might not otherwise know about. They can discuss your investments with the insight and nuance gained from working with individuals at all different levels of experience and understanding. They can help you optimize your portfolio, keep you on track, coach you through the tough times and commend your ultimate success.

Many different kinds of professionals make up the universe of advisers. There are straight commission brokers, who earn a fee on every trade you make. The more you trade, the better they do. There are fee-based professionals who will manage your portfolio for a small percentage of the assets in it. There are those who charge by the hour, like an attorney, and who will listen to your questions, assess your situation and provide advice. There are discretionary managers to whom you give the power to trade on your behalf, and there are arrangements in which you must give approval to every move up front.

Only you can decide which, if any, of these avenues might make sense for you. If you're more comfortable doing your own research (and there's plenty of information publicly available) and executing your own trades, by all means do so. If you're the kind of person who would appreciate a professional point of view, well, that's certainly available too.

Before you commit to any particular adviser, here are some questions you might want to ask him or her:

1.   What experience do you have?

How long has the planner been in practice? How much experience does she have helping individuals with their financial needs?

2.   What are your qualifications?

Look for a planner who has proven experience in investments or retirement planning. Ask what licenses and certifications the planner holds, and what steps he takes to stay current with changes in the field. If the planner holds a financial planning designation or certification, you can check on his background with the Certified Financial Planner Board or other relevant professional organizations.

The many kinds of advisers include Certified Financial Planners™, professional or CFP® practitioners, Certified Public Accountant-Personal Financial Specialists (CPA-PFS) and Chartered Financial Consultants (ChFC). Each of these titles indicates slightly different areas of specialization and degrees of study. The most important thing, though, is that the planner has the training and skill to provide assistance in your individual case, and that planner is someone with whom you feel comfortable.

3.   *What services do you offer?*

The services a financial planner offers depend on credentials, licenses and areas of expertise. Some planners offer advice on a range of topics but do not sell financial products. Others may provide advice only in specific areas, such as estate planning, tax matters or insurance.

4.   *What is your approach to financial planning?*

Make sure the planner's viewpoint is neither too cautious nor too aggressive for you. Some planners require you to have a certain net worth before offering services. Find out if the planner will carry out the financial recommendations developed for you or refer you to others who will.

Most planners will ask many of the questions we've asked here. They'll want to know your goals, your risk tolerance, your personal, family and business situation. The degree of customization they offer in their planning may vary.

Some planners take a holistic approach, looking at the totality of a client's financial life—insurance, taxes, estate planning and more. Others focus exclusively on a single area, such as portfolio management. Still others put clients with similar goals, investment time horizons or wealth levels into the same "basket" of securities—essentially, model portfolios in which a few sizes fit all (as we showed last chapter). You may have to meet with several planners before you find one with the appropriate "fit" for you. Take the time to get it right.

5.   Will you be the only person working with me?

The financial planner may work with you himself or have others assist him. You'll want to meet everyone who will be working with you. If the planner works with professionals outside his own practice (such as attorneys, insurance agents or tax specialists), get a list of their names to check on their backgrounds.

6.   How do you charge for your services?

As part of your financial planning agreement, the planner should clearly tell you in writing how she will be compensated for the services to be provided. As we've noted, it can be via salary from the planner's company, fees, hourly rates, commissions or a combination of any and all of the above.

7. *How much do you typically charge?*

While the amount you pay the planner will depend on your particular needs, the financial planner should be able to provide you with a cost estimate based on the work to be performed.

8. *Are there any potential conflicts of interest in our working together?*

Financial planners who sell insurance policies, securities or mutual funds have a business relationship with the companies that provide these products. The planner may also receive business for referring you to an insurance agent, accountant or attorney. There's nothing necessarily bad in these arrangements; it's simply that if they exist, the planner should inform you of them.

9. *What professional organizations do you belong to?*

Several government and professional organizations, such as FINRA (formerly NASD), your state insurance and securities departments, and Certified Financial Planner Board keep records on financial planners and advisers. Contact these groups to conduct a background check.

There's nothing unusual in performing these checks so, please, make the calls. The planner herself may provide references for you. After all, if she's helped others succeed in the markets, isn't that a good advertisement? Conversely, if you hear damaging stories from past customers or a professional organization, you'll want to proceed with caution, if at all.

10.   Can I have it in writing?

Ask the planner for a written agreement that details the services to be provided. Keep this document in your files for future reference.

By the way, a good planner will tell you most of these things without your having to ask. And almost all planners and advisers will meet with you for an introductory consultation—usually lasting about an hour—at no charge. All you'll invest, initially, is your time.

$$$ WHAT DID WE LEARN? $$$

1.   Every investor is different.

Your portfolio should reflect your individual objectives and goals at a level of risk comfortable for you. It doesn't matter what others may do—it's your future and it's your call.

2.   Portfolio risk tolerance is largely a function of age.

The more years you have until you'll need the money in your portfolio, the more volatility you can accept. With a longer time frame, you improve your chances for returns that meet historical long-term averages.

3.   The more asset classes, the greater the diversification.

By incorporating different kinds of domestic and international stocks, bonds and alternative assets in your portfolio, you increase the chances of steady returns and give yourself access to a wider range of opportunities.

4. *Rebalancing is key to staying on track.*

Review your portfolio quarterly. Rebalance it once a year to keep it consistent with your objectives. Reviewing and rebalancing are the "brushing and flossing," if you will, that will keep your portfolio working hard for you.

5. Professional financial planning can help you succeed.

A good financial planner—a knowledgeable individual who understands you as a person—can bring skills to bear in helping you build for the future.

Coming up...

One step to go. With a great plan in place, all that's left is to get ready for retirement.

8 | KICKING BACK IN RETIREMENT

C hances are, your attitude toward retirement will be shaped by your age. In your 20s and 30s, the concept is likely to seem pretty remote, something you know about but needn't pay much attention to. In your 40s, the idea probably starts to carry more weight. By your 50s, I'm told, retirement starts to seem like something pleasant that might actually happen to you.

But then, for too many people, retirement recedes like a horizon. As you draw closer, it moves farther away. You reach the age that should have been the starting line, but the comfortable years they talked about on TV are nowhere to be found. What happened?

There's no mystery. The retirement we'll have is a function of how well we've planned for it. If you leave it to chance, you might as well forget about it. So it's time to start thinking about it now.

I'm not suggesting you send away for brochures on assisted-living facilities, but I am saying you should start to consider some of the issues that will be important to you.

Here are a few pointers that can help as you begin to think about your eventual retirement.

1.   Save as much as you can as early as you can.

Though it's never too late to start, the sooner you begin saving, the more time your money has to grow. Gains each year build on the prior year's—that's the power of compounding, and the best way to accumulate wealth. At www.money.cnn.com/retirement/tools, you can find calculators that will let you see how quickly compounded money will grow.

2.   Set realistic goals.

Project your retirement expenses based on your needs, not what somebody else thinks. Be honest about how you want to live in retirement and how much it will cost. Then calculate how much you'll have to save to supplement Social Security and other sources of retirement income.

One rule of thumb is that you'll need 80 percent of your annual pre-retirement income to live comfortably. That might be enough if you've paid off your mortgage and are in excellent health when you kiss the office goodbye.

But if you plan to build your dream house, trot around the globe, or get that Ph.D. in philosophy you've always wanted, you may need 100 percent of your income or more. Again, the calculators at <u>www.money.cnn.com/retirement/tools</u> can show you how much you'll have to accumulate in order to live as you choose in retirement.

Remember, too, that your health care expenses are likely to go up in retirement, if only because you'll be paying more for insurance.

3.   Tax advantaged accounts represent an excellent way to save for retirement.

As we discussed early on, money contributed to a 401(k) grows tax-deferred. You don't pay taxes on it until you withdraw it. And Individual Retirement Accounts (IRAs), which come in a variety of flavors, also shelter your investment money while it grows.

A 401(k), offered by your employer, is likely to have fewer investment choices than an IRA. On the other hand, your employer will often match a portion of your contribution. It's a great deal.

An IRA has very few restrictions on the investments you can own. If you can afford it, it's a good idea to supplement a 401(k) with an IRA. The opportunity for compound, tax-deferred growth is a gift.

Regular contributions to either of these plans, plus time to let them grow, is likely to give you the money to enjoy a healthy and happy retirement for many years.

5.   Focus on your asset allocation more than on individual picks.

You know this already, right? As we've learned, the way you divide your portfolio between stocks, bonds and other asset classes will have the biggest impact on your long-term returns.

It will be much more important than the individual stocks and bonds you own, or when you buy and sell.

6. *Stocks are best for long-term growth.*

Stocks have the best chance of achieving high returns over long periods. We know this, and we know they're also the most volatile asset class. But a healthy dose will help ensure that your savings grow faster than inflation, increasing the purchasing power of your nest egg. Remember, it's best to own mutual funds, index funds and ETFs—not individual stocks.

7. *Don't move too heavily into bonds, even in retirement.*

This is an excellent point to remember. As you approach retirement age, of course you'll shift more into bonds. But even in retirement, which can last a few decades, it pays to maintain a healthy dose of stocks (maybe upwards of 50 percent in your 70s, and up to 30 percent in your 80s). Many retirees stash most of their portfolio in bonds for the income. Unfortunately, over 10 to 15 years, inflation easily can erode the purchasing power of bonds' interest payments.

8. *Tax-efficient withdrawals can stretch the life of your nest egg.*

Once you hit retirement, you get to kick back and enjoy your savings. But you'll enjoy them a lot more and a lot longer if you manage your withdrawals smartly. To give yourself the best chance of outliving your money, financial experts recommend you withdraw no more than 4 percent to 5 percent of your total nest egg every year.

You also want to minimize your tax bite. Generally speaking, the more money you leave tax-deferred in a 401(k) or IRA, the more your nest egg will grow, because a large balance can compound faster without the drag of taxes. But taxes will eventually come due on that money.

9.   *Working part-time in retirement can help in more ways than one.*

Working keeps you socially engaged and reduces the amount of your nest egg you must withdraw annually once you retire.

Imagine taking a part-time job that reduces your withdrawals from an IRA by $15,000 a year for 10 years. By letting that money grow tax-deferred longer, after 10 years you would have almost $220,000 that you otherwise wouldn't have had, assuming you earn an 8 percent annual return.

10.   *Find other creative ways to get more mileage out of retirement assets.*

For instance, you might consider relocating to an area with lower living expenses. Doing so could stretch your retirement income by 15 percent or more.

While there are many effective strategies for building a comfortable retirement, the most important steps are planning and action. Don't put either off another day.

$$$ WHAT DID WE LEARN? $$$

1. The most important step to retirement is planning for it.

It's an old saying, but those who fail to plan are planning to fail. A good retirement doesn't just happen. It's the payoff for many years of steady, disciplined investing.

2. Take advantage of retirement savings accounts.

An IRA and 401(k) plan let you earn money in tax-deferred, protected havens. They're among the best deals you're likely to get in life.

3. Don't underestimate your living expenses in retirement.

Many people assume their expenses will drop to nothing once they retire. But in truth, figure you'll need at least 80 percent of your pre-retirement income. Social security will cover part of that, and you may have a pension that will provide more. But you'll have to make up the rest yourself. Keep that fact in mind when you invest.

4. Keep stocks in your portfolio—you may need the performance.

While it's natural to invest more conservatively as we age, remember that today's retirement can last 30 years or more. You'll still need the growth that only stocks can provide.

5. ***The biggest risk is doing nothing.***

   That's pretty clear, isn't it? Make it happen.

9 | YOUR NEXT STEPS

"Above all, try something."

– Franklin Delano Roosevelt (1882-1945)

L et's be clear about one thing: we're in one of those odd times when almost nothing you could have done would have given you a positive return from the stock market in 2008. No matter how your assets were allocated, no matter how diversified you were, no matter what stocks you owned, you were fated to lose money.

Maybe a few people got out of the market in time to avoid the tsunami. But most of us—and I include myself here— stayed in and took it. With a long-term plan, there's really no other choice. And having stayed with me through the past eight chapters, I hope you'll agree that long-term investing is the most logical and sensible way to grow your money.

I wrote this book to provide you with the tools to establish a safe, sound investment plan based on proven principles. In no way is this book sufficient to make you an expert investor, a sure-fire stock picker, a brilliant day trader or a prescient market timer (actually, the last three don't really exist).

Just because you can bake a pie doesn't make you Martha Stewart, and you'll need more than a stick and a pair of skates to be Wayne Gretzky. It will take more than this book to turn you into Warren Buffett.

On the other hand, you've seen that the world of investing is knowable. It's not magic, and it's not filled with arcane secrets revealed only to the high priests. It's logical, endlessly fascinating and a worthy subject for both study and participation.

The financial markets are the place where the panoply of human activity gets quantified, and we're all invited to take part. The markets allow anyone with desire and a little cash to have a role—however small—in building the world. Through our investments, we can help clean energy companies get off the ground, construct schools and hospitals in remote areas, or be part of a company that's connecting the whole planet through wireless technology.

Okay, I know it sounds a bit grandiose, but that doesn't mean it isn't true. Not only can we be a part of all that activity, we can make money on it. And not only do we make money, but the projects and companies we fund can operate for moral, as well as economic, benefit. I'll bet you never thought of the financial markets that way before.

Finance and investing have been around for thousands of years. Archaeologists working in Mesopotamia have found clay tablets with cuneiform writing that state how much grain was to be paid to the king on a future date. It's a long way from those tablets to the nightly business report on CNN, but the idea's the same. Only the transmission system has changed.

Right now, we've been beat up pretty good. Everything hurts. Comparisons to the Great Depression of the 1930s aren't really accurate, but no other analogy comes close to describing the pain, the systemic failures and the sense of crisis gripping government, Wall Street and the public at large.

It's as though we've been punched without warning. We're more or less over the initial shock, the kind that has your brain sending signals to all your body parts to make sure they're still there. Now the slow, dull ache begins. It's going to take a while to get over it, but get over it we will. We always have.

The world is a forward-looking place. For every bubble— from Holland's tulip mania in the 17th century to our tech bubble early in the 21st—there have been a thousand stories of steady growth. For every Enron there are ten Microsofts. And as long as people have the freedom to strive, there will always be more.

Your job is to take the tools you're given and make something. In this case, your future. It's time to use the power of the investing principles to set up your own wealth-building plan. You can establish your IRA, pay off your credit card debt, construct a portfolio and make regular contributions to it. You can allocate your assets to achieve proper diversification, or you can seek the assistance of a financial professional to help you. You can take advantage of tax-saving accounts and evaluate opportunities against objective criteria.

Once you start, you'll be surprised at how easily diligence becomes second nature and how quickly your assets accumulate. With a map in your hands, the path becomes much clearer.

At the beginning of this book, I noted that you were taking a first step toward building your financial future. You've now come a long way. If you apply the lessons we've learned with discipline and consistency, I have every confidence in your ultimate success.

BIBLIOGRAPHY

END NOTES: Cited works

1   Di Pasquale, Denise and Edward L. Glaeser. "Incentives and Social Capital: Are Homeowners Better Citizens?" Academic Press, 1999.

2   "Zakaria: A More Disciplined America." Newsweek.com.

3   "Negative Equity," *The New York Times*, February 2, 2008.

4   Woolsey, Ben and Matt Schulz. "Credit card industry facts, debt statistics 2006–2008." (Source: Federal Reserve Bulletin, February 2006 and myfico.com), CreditCards.com.

5   "Changes in Food Costs Covered by Welfare Grant, 1990-2008," Hunger Action Network of New York State.

6   "The Global 2000," Forbes, April 4, 2008.

7 Ibbotson Associates. "Stocks, Bonds, Bills and Inflation Yearbook, 2007," Morningstar.

8 Ibid.

Other sources

"10 Questions to Ask When Choosing a Financial Planner," Certified Financial Planner Board of Standards, Inc., 2008.

"Make Sure Your Financial Planner is Not a Loser," Free Money Finance, February 2, 2006.

Mann, Bill. "Why You Must Own International Stocks," The Motley Fool, February 19, 2008.

ETFZone.com